We Are Not Users

Dialogues, Diversity, and Design

Eswaran Subrahmanian, Yoram Reich, and Sruthi Krishnan

The MIT Press
Cambridge, Massachusetts
London, England

This book was set in ITC Stone Serif Std and ITC Stone Sans Std by Toppan Best-set Premedia Limited. Printed and bound in the United States of America.

Library of Congress Cataloging-in-Publication Data

Names: Subrahmanian, Eswaran, author. | Reich, Yoram, author. | Krishnan, Sruthi, author.
Title: We are not users : dialogues, diversity, and design / Eswaran Subrahmanian, Yoram Reich, and Sruthi Krishnan.
Description: Cambridge, MA : The MIT Press, 2020.
    Includes bibliographical references and index.
Identifiers: LCCN 2019008961 | ISBN 9780262043366 (hardcover : alk. paper)
Subjects: LCSH: Design.
Classification: LCC NK1510 .S83 2020 | DDC 745.4--dc23 LC record available at
    https://lccn.loc.gov/2019008961

10 9 8 7 6 5 4 3 2 1

To all those who shaped and contributed to the ideas in this book, including designing, our mentor and muse

Contents

Acknowledgments

We would like to acknowledge first and foremost Arthur Westerberg for being a founding member of the *n*-dim project and teaching us that child-like curiosity does not have to be lost when you grow older and become famous. Without Art, there would be no *n*-dim project. We thank him for financially supporting this effort in the creation of this book and for legitimizing us with those who did not see design in the way we did in the academic community. We thank Steve Fenves, Sarosh Talukdar, Arthur Westerberg, and many others for having had the vision in 1976 to create the first Design Research Center (DRC) (1976 to 1986) at Carnegie Mellon University based on Herbert A. Simon's book *The Sciences of the Artificial* and the subsequent National Science Foundation Engineering Design Research Center (NSF EDRC) (1986 to 1997) crafted by some of the same people. They provided the space for a multidisciplinary understanding of design and supported it to enhance the practice of design continuously for over fifteen years. We thank the directors of the NSF EDRC—Fritz Prinz, Dan Siewiorek, Sarosh Talukdar, and Art Westerberg—who always encouraged exploring design with our approach.

We would like to thank John Gallagher, who brought the problem of supporting the entirety of designing to us in 1987, along with James Easter, Bill Elm, and Emily Roth of the then Westinghouse Electric Corporation. We thank Asmund Maeland of ABB, who provided us the opportunity to study the design of a number of electric power generation and distribution products. We also would like to thank many of the people who over the years contributed to this project directly or indirectly, including Ray Betler, Bob Di Silvestro, and Curt McCullers of Bombardier Corporation (previously ADTRANZ); Diane Rishel, Mary Downs, and Reed Green of Alcoa; Thomas Schwab, Andrea Jahnke, Harald Mackamul, and Johannes Maier of

Robert Bosch; Judith Spering of Boeing; and many others who participated in the *n*-dim group discussions, workshops, and retreats.

We thank the Design Theory special interest group at MINES ParisTech and the people behind it—Armand Hatchuel, Pascal Le Masson, and Benoit Weil—for the last ten years of dialogues and collaborative work on design theory and the role of design in and across many disciplines. They provided us with the space for expanding our dialogue and the privilege of spending a week every year in Paris.

We would like to express our thanks to the corporations that funded us and gave us confidence that we were looking at the right problem. Other funding entities that provided small and large contributions have included ABB, ADTRANZ/Bombardier, Air Products, ALCOA, Boeing, Bosch, CMU NSF Engineering Design Research Center, DARPA Made Program, DuPont, Ford, National Institute of Standards and Technology, National Science Foundation (NSF), Pennsylvania Infrastructure and Technology Alliance (PITA), and Westinghouse Electric.

We thank Fields of View and its architects Bharath M. Palavalli and Harsha Krishna. The ideas in the book have been nourished and honed with the work done at Fields of View.

Agatha Christie, the queen of English detective fiction, wrote that when she was asked "Where do you get your ideas from?" she felt tempted to say, "I always go to Harrods" or give a similarly snappy reply. Explaining the creative process is something artists rarely like to do, and that is why we consider ourselves privileged to have had the opportunity to understand how the dance production *Samhara* was choreographed. We wish to thank the artistic director of Nrityagram Dance Ensemble, Surupa Sen, for her patience and generosity in sharing her thoughts and time. And we wish to thank Heshma Wignaraja, artistic director of Chitrasena Dance Company, for taking the time for an interview.

We wish to thank all the partners of Design across Cultures, a cross-cultural design collaboration between Fields of View in Bangalore and MediaLAB Amsterdam and send a special note of thanks to all the alumni who participated in the program.

We wish to thank Smita Khanna for her editorial feedback and Namrata Mehta for the design of the visuals in the book.

We thank the following people who read an earlier version of the book and provided us with valuable comments and encouragement: Margareta

Norell Bergendahl, Peter R. N. Childs, Steven J. Fenves, Armand Hatchuel, Robin Ann King, Pascal Le Masson, Guru Madhavan, Sebastiaan Meijer, Ram Sriram, Shyam Sunder, Runhua Tan, and Arthur Westerberg.

I, Yoram Reich, thank the School of Mechanical Engineering at Tel Aviv University for providing the space and freedom for my participation in the project since 1993; my late friend and colleague Offer Shai for endless discussions on design and other diverse disciplines in the last twenty years; my parents for nurturing my foundations for designing a better world; my children, Shaked and Clil, for posing challenging problems; and Nurit for brightening the context.

As the song goes, "I get by with a little help from my friends." And in this case, it was more, much more—so much more. For me, Sruthi Krishnan, this book would not have been possible without this constellation of support—Sridhar for spirited digressions; Nivi, friend, counselor, and sanctuary; the rockstars of Nrityagram—Surupa, Bijayini, and Lynne—the women whose lives are a testament to that elusive spirit we all seek; Geethu for those carefully timed breaks, chai, and conversations; my father for telling me stories; and Koma for being more of a friend than mother.

Thanking all of those who have shaped our thoughts and provided support would take an entire chapter. This list of n-dim group members is just a sample. I, Eswaran Subrahmanian, would like to thank especially Sarosh Talukdar, who as director of DRC hired me, mentored me at the Design Research Center that preceded EDRC, and got me interested in design. I am grateful for having learned curiosity from my father, a sense of social welfare and the drive to learn languages from my mother, the need to read from my brother Kannan, and the ability to find ways to be creative from my younger brother, Hari. The late Suresh Konda was a close friend, mentor, colleague, and master chef who often kept many of the people in the group fed on food and discussions in my house and created a sense of a true salon. We miss him dearly even today. Thanks to Bharath and Harsha and the team at Fields of View for creating the space for exploring the role of inclusive design in people's lives. Finally, I am grateful for Robin, who was always amused by my obsession with design and brought articles of interest, and my son, Amartya, who still does not believe that his father would ever finish this book.

We are delighted that the book found a home with the MIT Press, and it seems especially appropriate to be working with the Press on the fiftieth anniversary of Herbert Simon's *The Sciences of the Artificial*. We are grateful to our editor Douglas Sery and the rest of the team at the MIT Press, Noah Springer, Jermey Matthews, Deborah Cantor-Adams, and all others who cared for the book. And we wish to thank the anonymous reviewers of the book whose feedback and comments sharpened our focus.

Writing a book seems like living a lifetime in the span of a few years. There are many whose conversations, care, and critique shaped the book, and we are grateful to all of them.

1   The Prisoner's Song

"Prisoner, tell me who was it that wrought this unbreakable chain?"
"It was I," said the prisoner, "who forged this chain very carefully."
—Rabindranath Tagore, "Prisoner," in *Gitanjali*

The Human-Made

The Krishnagiri region in South India was given the status of a district more than a decade ago. Several development initiatives were already underway in the area, which had once been dominated by forests and verdant mountains. Indeed, its forested terrain had been one of the reasons the district posed a challenge to the administration.

On an afternoon in January 2008, the area's forest officer sat on his chair looking at the young journalists-to-be who had gathered around him to tour and report on Krishnagiri as part of their coursework. On one of his office walls was a map covered with green splotches that represented forests and gray splotches that represented dense human settlements. Huge swathes of gray dominated the map and were interrupted by tiny slivers of green. "Once upon a time," the forest officer began, "the entire map was covered with green. Now this is all that's left."

What the forest officer said was not surprising. If we had a map that showed how the earth has changed over time, it would be similar to the map that told the story of Krishnagiri. The green world of nature and forests has shrunk slowly, and the gray world created by us humans has expanded and steadily encroached on the green.

We humans have always tried to shape the spaces we occupy and live in, and the scale of this endeavor continues to increase. From the wheel, invented during the time when we inhabited caves, to the latest smartphone, we have continuously tried to change the world around us by creating different artifacts. The difference between the world characterized by green and the world signified by gray lies in the extent to which these human-made artifacts dominate the landscape.

Look around you. Objects, articles, items, products, and goods are artifacts that populate the material environment and mediate our sensory experiences, from the mundane to the marvelous. You can swipe the screen of a smartphone, see movies while flying in an airplane, hear the daily miracle of water flowing from a tap inside your home, chug milk from a bottle, and breathe into your pillow as you snuggle and fall asleep.

The reign of artifacts is not limited to what you can sense and experience; it extends to the realm of the abstract, too. The signs and symbols we have created help us communicate and bring concepts to reality. The services that we have conceptualized and implemented include hospitals, schools, electrical systems, water networks, and agricultural supply chains that deliver food to us. Even the policies that govern us, the constitution that binds us, and the laws and legislations that determine our rights and responsibilities were decided on by us. Whether we live in Bangalore, Beijing, Beirut, Boston, or Buenos Aires, we share a common citizenship of belonging to this world of artifacts. We are the ones who gave birth to it.

We humans are the ones who etch cityscapes in concrete. We organize ourselves into communities now governed by carefully worded constitutions. We negotiate markets and formulate rules and regulations to govern them. We compose codas and binary code. We pave invisible pathways to make electrons help us converse and formulate policies, even this paragraph. We have shaped every aspect of our existence—this world where we breathe, fall in love, and raise our children, the stage where we enact our rites of passage. This environment, this world of artifacts, is our creation. It is human-made.

The human-made and the humans for whom it is made—who determine the purpose or need, who make it, who live with it, and who will inherit it—share a complex relationship. In this book, we attempt to uncover different layers of that relationship and in some sense to forge it afresh. But why should we bother in the first place? In this chapter, we attempt to answer that question.

The Unseen Web

In 2006, *Time* magazine declared "You" as the person of the year. "Yes, you. You control the Information Age. Welcome to your world," it declared reassuringly. Every individual is a user, and the human-made world is there to do the user's bidding, to help each person lead a "better" life. You have better healthcare, education, and life-expectancy rates. You can travel faster and communicate instantaneously, and the next handheld wonder is just a nanoprocessor away. You can have smoother skin, become smarter, and wear a gadget that will make you healthier by counting every single step you take. It is all at your service. You are the master, and these things are puppets performing for your pleasure. Stronger, faster, smoother, better, safer, simpler: isn't this what artifacts are meant for?

All this is based on two interrelated assumptions—that humans and the world they have created share a one-way relationship of utility and that all humans are users.

Let us tackle these assumptions. Consider a social media site such as Facebook or Twitter. Everyone on Facebook and Twitter is considered a user—someone who uses a service. In the case of Facebook, the service the platform provides is connecting people together. In the case of Twitter, the service the platform provides is allowing you talk to the world and see what others are talking about. The platform and the people are joined by a one-way relationship of utility: the platform provides a service, and people use that service. But is that really the case?

When people's online profiles are mined to provide targeted information to influence voting decisions, the relationship of people to these platforms is not just that of use. It is political. When false information that is spread through the platform puts people's lives in danger, how should we talk about the risks in the relationship? When trolls on the platform target journalists who are critical of the government to the point that the journalists start fearing for their lives, how should we describe the relationship between the person and the platform?

The one-way relationship of utility then becomes a poor way to describe the relationship between the platform, different kinds of people, government, and politics. We are all not users. We are journalists, politicians, activists, voters, dissidents, trolls, children, and parents, and we see and experience the platform differently. The different positions we hold and diverse perspectives we have cannot be flattened into one homogeneous entity called user.

We share a complex relationship with the human-made, and utility is just one of the numerous strands that bind us with artifacts. The relationship is more like a node in a web. The *-er* words (such as *better*, *stronger*, and *faster*) throw a veil over the interconnectedness, the web of diverse relationships that enmesh us within the world of the human-made.

An artifact like a social media platform affects people's lives and choices. And people's lives and choices decide its fate. An online platform then has to concern itself not just with how fast a video can load but also with politics, culture, economics, and power. The notion of limitless electronic vistas can be transformed into online real estate if the legislation being proposed to govern the internet is considered. Domain names such as .beauty and .book will be auctioned to the highest bidder. Questions of surveillance, privacy, and memory are being debated at dining tables, in classrooms, and in legislative halls. Censorship is not a theoretical concept anymore. It is not that this web of laws, legislations, economics, and politics has suddenly been woven into the online space. It is just that we are not always cognizant of this web. Every artifact around you, whether a road or a digital platform, is enmeshed within an unseen web of complex relationships with different kinds of people.

Let us take another example. Every visitor to Bangalore marvels at and mulls over the city's traffic congestion. Signal-free corridors or roads without any traffic lights are seen as a way to address congestion. The relationship of utility in this situation is fairly easy to describe: drivers use the signal-free road to drive their cars faster. Now, instead of seeing the relationship between corridor and driver as a one-way relationship of utility, let us try to describe the web of relationships the signal-free corridor shares with different kinds of people.

Although the signal-free corridor has been built using taxpayer money, pedestrians cannot use it much because it is dangerous to walk on such roads with cars whizzing past them at high speeds. Environmentalists who advocate for more public transportation do not like these corridors because public buses mostly do not use these corridors, given that buses find it difficult to make stops in them. Some of these corridors have a toll, and private cab owners have protested against hikes in the toll, making the road a site of conflict between the government and private cab owners.

With any artifact, a web made of social, political, economic, and cultural threads is always there. It is just that sometimes ignorance is bliss, and we choose not to see the web. When deciding to buy a smartphone, are you really interested in the antecedents of each of its parts? Maybe it was manufactured using child labor. Perhaps it uses metal from mines that are destroying ecologically sensitive areas. When you buy a diaper, do you really want the image of landfills to clog your head?

Sometimes the web seems intractable. How would we have thought of speed without the clock, which sliced our lives into measurable chunks? And if every tick is counting down, the economic rollercoaster, the Fukushima nuclear reactor failure, food insecurity, and agrarian crises are but a few of the human-made disasters we face. A badly crafted chair can hurt your back; a polluted city worsens your child's respiratory problems; a mismanaged city means scarce water, long stressful drives, and mosquitoes that cause diseases. A platform that connects friends and allows them to share pictures of cute cats can influence the outcome of elections in a democracy.

The one-way relationship of utility obfuscates this complex relationship we share with the world we have created. There is a rising dissonance as we refuse to see and grapple with the complex relationship between us and the world we have created. This rising dissonance screams that the dialogue between us, the material world of our creation, and the natural world lies broken.

We do acknowledge the dissonance, the rift between us and the world of our creation. Every discipline—whether technology, social science, political science, or economics—has its own perspective and its own to-do list of things that can address these issues. It is as though despite plumbing the depths of different disciplines, something is still missing. We seem unable to breach disciplinary boundaries and together articulate the complexity of the world we have created in order to grapple with it.

There is one field that is acutely aware of this unseen web binding us, the material world of our creation, and the natural world. This is a field that is supposed to act as a bridge between different disciplines and the world of our making. It is a field whose primary concern is that making. All the verbs we used before—*shaping, crafting, composing, creating, building, engineering, fashioning, manufacturing, constructing*—all these can be substituted by this one word, *designing*.

The human-made—including material artifacts, signs and symbols, services, processes, and environments—are all outcomes of designing, a human instinct to craft and control. We have sculpted the world we inhabit extensively, and what ails us is a dissonance of our own making. The dialogue between us—the one between the material world of our creation and the natural world—lies broken because the dialogue in *designing* this world of our creation is broken.

Dissonance in Designing

Designers have the power to change and remake the world, which is both a powerful and frustrating realization. The radical possibilities that designing offers are not often understood, much less practiced. Often designing is viewed through a narrow lens as utilitarian, merely ornamental, or even esoteric, an almost mystical act.

Designing is not just about utility; it has political, social, and economic significance. Designing is not decoration; it is bringing together aesthetics, art, technology, science, social sciences, and diverse other disciplines to inquire into the world critically and remake it. Designing is not only about the "Aha" moment; it is about a process that involves people.

People are not the same everywhere. Their likes, dislikes, customs, concerns, history, needs, and responses differ depending on where they come from, who they are, and what they want to do. Some of us are young, and some are old. Some are artists, industrialists, teachers, journalists, politicians, mothers, soldiers, farmers, activists, teachers, architects. We can claim different epithets. We occupy different positions of power and privilege. We see the world in diverse ways. These differences are crucial when we design. How, then, can we reimagine designing in a way that people are not reduced to being mere users but become a part of the process—active participants in the designing and creation of an artifact?

Different approaches to designing deal with similar themes—a focus on people; the importance of the social, participation, and context-specificity; a wider notion of what designing encompasses, where designing is a transdisciplinary/interdisciplinary field. But something is missing in all of these approaches.

Some attempts at understanding designing formalize design to such an extent that they offer little relevance for practice. Others provide to-do lists and frameworks for practitioners but lack the theoretical base that allows for a systematic building of knowledge that can develop into a mature field of study. There remains a gap between theory and practice, and what we need is a conception of designing that can build a bridge across both.

We need designing to be the field it was imagined to be—a field of study that embraces disciplinary diversity and draws from science, engineering and technology, social sciences, philosophy, and art. Designing needs to be reclaimed as a field of practice where people are the focus, where different perspectives can come together and shape the world. Designing has the potential to be a liberal art, but it is not one. Why not?

Our answer is that there is a lack of respect for diversity. Designing needs diversity like humans need the five elements.[1] Designing is about bringing together diverse people, perspectives, actors, or stakeholders—whatever you choose to call them. Designing has to draw from different disciplines. Can you imagine a car being built using only the principles of physics? Designing a car needs physics, arts, infrastructural considerations, engineering principles, economics, and marketing magic. Being a designer is about being aware of and able to employ such diversity. It is about bringing together analytical, creative, interpersonal, and humane approaches to making.

Diversity is a valuable asset to have, but it is difficult to grapple with. Most approaches to designing try to box diversity into fixed categories with classic one-size-fits-all or universal solutions. For example, people from all cultures are simplistically labeled users. Or diversity is reduced to manageable sizes. Even though designing is beyond the scope of such parochial categorizations, it is often limited to being just a science, an art, or an embodiment of the latest buzzword. There is dissonance in designing today because we designers continue to struggle with diversity.

Designing, Diversity, and Dialogue

Instead of trying to struggle with diversity or trying to tame it, can we embrace it? Celebrate diversity? Our answer is, "Yes, we can." When we think about designing with a diverse set of people at its center, we have a complex dance. It is simultaneously about the individual and the social, the particular and the universal. It is simultaneously so because it focuses not on one convenient end but instead on the connections between them, the dynamics between them, the dialogue between them. Can designing be conceived of as a dialogue?

The principle of dialogue allows us to conceptualize designing as an act enriched by diversity—whether disciplinary diversity or a diversity of perspectives. A dialogue focuses our attention on the context, providing an alternative for a one-size-fits-all paradigm. A dialogue is about collaboration. It requires a coming together of different disciplines, perspectives, theories, and practices.

We need a fresh dialogue in designing that lets us welcome and respect multiple voices. Such a dialogue needs a new language that accommodates plurality—that does not impose one view but allows for multiple views.

In this book, we present the building blocks of a language that conceives designing in all its richness—that provides the base for a theoretical model and also illuminates different contexts of practice. What we have attempted is a synthesis, drawing from diverse disciplines to weave them into a model for understanding and practicing designing. We join others in asking that designing be practiced and studied as a liberal art. What we offer in this book is a foundation for designing to assume that mantle.

We Are Not Users is a call to anyone who designs—professionals, academics in the field of design, and everyone interested in the field of design—to reclaim and rethink the field so that it is more ethical and humane.

Organization of the Book

First, we need to understand the history of the study of designing. Most books offer a strand of this history, either from a particular subfield (visual design, graphic design) or a focus on artifacts (the history of the pencil or the engine). Because we are interested in designing in all its richness, we need to start by looking at how designing has been studied across the ages, which is what we do in chapter 2, A Very Short History of Designing. The chapter proceeds chronologically, beginning with the wheel in the eighth century BC and journeying through different moments in history up to the present.

Unlike other narratives of history related to designing, we draw from different fields, including architecture, industrial design, engineering design, and management. Even though people in different fields of study are now interested in designing, each field is struggling to articulate a cogent theoretical base that will allow for systematic knowledge building and be relevant to practice. Chapter 2 essentially builds a shared memory of designing—a shared corpus of knowledge that draws from different strands of designing. Chapter 2 ends with questions that contemporary understanding of designing is struggling with.

Using the questions raised in chapter 2 that existing approaches to understanding designing contend with as a starting point, we build our alternative conception of designing in chapter 3, We the Designers. Existing approaches to designing face key issues related to people and context. Failures that result from a one-size-fits-all approach stem from not taking into account people and context. The reason that different approaches do not take into account context is that it involves diversity—diversity of perspectives in designing and in the complexities of synthesizing different disciplines in the process of designing. Conceiving designing in all its interconnected diverse richness requires an alternative frame.

In order to develop that alternative conception, we use the principle of dialogue. In chapter 3, we explain in detail the principle of dialogue—what we mean by the dialogue—which sets the base for developing our model of designing, called the shared memory of designing, and begin introducing the vocabulary that underpins the model. In figure 1.1, we provide an overview of the shared memory of designing model and the different terms that form the vocabulary of expressing our alternative conception of designing. The numbers shown in the image below indicate the chapters the different concepts are introduced in. (Appendix A, A Vocabulary for Designing, includes all the terms introduced in the book for easy reference.)

A new way of designing needs a new language. In chapter 4, A New Vocabulary, we start building the vocabulary that underpins our conception of designing. We speak to a choreographer who brought together two different dance forms in the spirit of a dialogue to create a new production. This process of creating a new language that can talk to two dance forms mirrors how the process of designing occurs.

In chapter 4, we take you through theories from cognitive science, linguistics, the sociology of work, and the ethnography of engineering work to explain our conception of designing. In doing so, we introduce the terms *boundary objects* and *models* in designing as the mediators and embodiment of the dialogue. By studying these mediators, we can understand how designing unfolds and how we can manage the process.

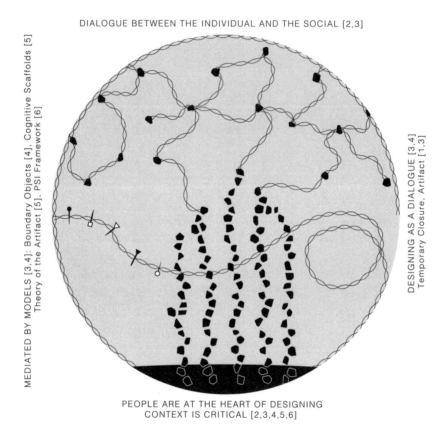

Figure 1.1
Our conception of designing. *Note:* Numbers in square brackets refer to chapters.

In chapter 5, Design Detritus, we look at the environmental and social costs of bad design and the ways that our approach helps address these concerns. We extend our vocabulary to include the *theory of the artifact* as a contextual theory continuously built and refined during the process of modeling. The theory of the artifact is a measure of the health of the process of designing. And we reintroduce shared memory as the living repository of the information associated with designing.

Chapter 6, Context, Context, Context, as the name suggests, is about context. Given that context is important in designing, how do we understand and characterize different contexts in which designing takes place? Chapter 6 deals with this question by introducing the PSI framework, which consists of problem space, social space, and institutional space. Traditionally, designing has been seen as professional practice, and the social, cultural, and political implications of designing are downplayed. The PSI framework provides both the language and the methods for bringing in context and the attendant social, cultural, and political dimensions of designing. We illustrate the PSI framework using different examples drawn from our case studies and research over the years.

Invariably, a prescription is expected at the end to answer the question, "What do I do with all this information?" Because dialogue is a dynamic and emergent act, it eludes prescription. Therefore, we shift our focus to examining the dialogue and the insights that we can bring in to examine the dialogue. We conclude chapter 6 with a set of questions that will help in probing the dialogue in designing.

There is nothing like perfect design because the idea of what is perfect keeps changing. Yet we do etch full stops in the sands of time—temporary closures, a refill before we resume the journey again, a slight intake of breath before continuing the song. A pause. Chapter 7, Designing Our Future, marks that pause.

A Temporary Closure

There are no guaranteed solutions to the complex problems we face. There are strong forces, powers that be, vested interests, and networks of intertwined complex factors that do not want diverse voices to be heard, much less have a dialogue. But feeling helpless in the face of an unexpected shower is quite different from feeling the same way about global warming, the economy, or your city. In this world of artifacts, human beings are the measure. There is none other. And as humans, we should be able to tackle what we have created.

No superhero can brandish a sword and sever complicated knots to liberate us. It is up to us, as citizens of this world we have created, to do what is needed. We are citizens who have not yet exercised fully our ability to shape this world. We are all designers. Anyone who is affected by this built environment has something of value to offer in changing it. Can we gather our diverse abilities for a rich and deep dialogue to design together? Can we create a new future that paves the way for a dialogue?

We do not know what the future will be like, but we can design it. It is not easy to achieve what we envisage—a vibrant dialogue to design the future. But every designing endeavor—where we unleash our powers of imagination and creativity to sculpt the unseen, script the unknown, and shape unborn ideas—starts with a dream. It is a dream built on hope, on the promise of a better tomorrow designed with all of us as free, fully participating citizens. In what way might that world be better than our current world? *We Are Not Users* is the start of a dialogue to design that idea of better.

2   A Very Short History of Designing

Every image embodies a way of seeing. Even a photograph. For photographs are not, as is often assumed, a mechanical record. Every time we look at a photograph, we are aware, however slightly, of the photographer selecting that sight from an infinity of other possible sights. This is true even in the most casual family snapshot.

—John Berger, *Ways of Seeing*

How would you write about the history of a city?

Would you talk about its streets? Unravel their grids? Mark locations that matured into landmarks, while accepting you can never name all of them? Perhaps you would speak about the people—those who claim it is their home, those who think they own it, or those unborn who will inherit it someday. What about those who have never seen the city yet know its shoreline and dream of it? Would they count? Where would you draw the city's boundaries? Can it be marked on land? Is it where the concrete kingdom narrows into an artery cutting across vast swaths of unmarked mud paths? Or is it elsewhere, limited and liberated by our collective memories?

While writing this chapter on the history of designing, we had similar questions, for designing is as complex and dynamic a muse as a city is. When there are many stories that can be told, how do we narrate one history? With these narrative threads constantly pulsing, where do we strike a pause?

For starters, what we have in this book is a history, not the history. We acknowledge that there can be multiple narratives, but we have chosen to focus on one. The events we have chosen and the ideas highlighted are all presented with the intent of building a foundation on which to structure other ideas—to prime a historical canvas onto which we will paint our contributions. Moreover, this narrative is not exhaustive. Our intent is not to look at every rock and pebble dotting the seashore but to cruise by to understand the path the shoreline has traversed.[1]

How will we approach our romp through history? We introduce here a key concept in our study of designing—shared memory, or the lens that informs our way of seeing the history of designing.

The House of Nine Muses

To explain what shared memory is, we'd like you to walk with us through a museum. The word *museum* draws its origins from the nine Muses revered by the ancient Greeks. Daughters of Mnemosyne, the personification of memory, and Zeus, the lord of the sky, these Muses inspire quests in literature, sciences, and the arts. This relationship is insightful: from memory springs the source of all knowledge. (This is not to say that there are no leaps and jumps; it is just to remind ourselves that all things new, including knowledge, have tenuous roots that stretch back in time.) We use the word *museum* not in the sense it is widely used and understood. Rather, we use it to mean simultaneously a museum, a library, and an archive. Let us call our museum the House of Nine Muses, which is a space for collective recording, remembering, and reflecting—a shared memory.

Assume our imaginary House of Nine Muses is a museum dedicated to a city. Now, let us revisit the question at the beginning of the chapter: "How would you write about the history of the city?" The answer would lie inside the House of Nine Muses.

If you want to write about the history of the city, you enter the House of Nine Muses with that intent. As you walk in through one of its many entrances, you will spot books, documents, parchments, scrolls, plaques, and tablets sitting alongside video tapes and audio recordings.

If your interest is in a specific period (say, the time when the city suffered from a drought), you may focus on laboriously typed notes on the measures the city council took to address the drought. You may come across detailed plans of how water was rationed by the department of water supply. You will also spend some time on the charts describing how to improve the city's groundwater levels.

If you are interested in the birds of the city, you may focus on the blueprints for a floating cage to house exotic birds in the city's zoo. You will notice that next to the blueprints are hand-drawn placards shouting "Free Wings," remnants of a protest against shutting birds inside cages.

Everything in the museum is a keeper of memory. Everything holds a story within. But what the story is, how the story progresses, what the plot points toward, and how the ending ought to be framed are for you to mull over and decide. It is as though everything in the museum is a prop and you are the director of the play. You can choose what roles each thing will play, what they will communicate and how, and whether they will have a say in the story. By doing so, you too become a part of the story. It has a trace that glistens with your choices.

For instance, if you wanted to tell the story of scarves in the city, you could first arrange specimens of different scarves stored in the second-floor corner room. You could then pull out sales figures from different stores and even records of the weather to underline the wild popularity of the red woolen scarves at a particular time every year. Biographies of artisan weavers could be stacked alongside rosters of auction houses. Tomes of laws debating the use of scarves could be displayed alongside instructions from fashionistas on how to drape them. A corner could be dedicated to a leading lady of the movies whose most memorable image was of her walking into the horizon with her signature chiffon scarf billowing in the wind.

You could weave different stories, all intertwined, a multithreaded braid. Every story has something more to tell you, a deeper insight, a broader view, a nuanced understanding of what is in the museum, how it came into being, and what it tells you. Each story is a history. In other words, there are as many histories that can be recounted as there are stories.

Your own home is one such museum.[2] All the objects you have—what you have displayed, what you have kept tucked away in old trunks and wrapped in covers lined with scented sachets—keep a record and tell a story. Look around you. Everything you see—whether street lamps, cars, canals, or exchange rates—is connected. These things all hold stories, and longer ones have episodes. These different stories continue to unfold and interweave, even as you read this page. The city, your street, and your home are part of a living, breathing museum.

Shared Memory

The museum houses the shared memory. It is what allows us to understand what has been designed—the artifact—whether a scarf or a city. If we wanted to understand scarves, we would examine the shared memory associated with the scarves. If we wanted to understand the city, we would examine the entire museum. Essentially,

Understanding (artifact) = Examining (shared memory of the artifact)

Using the same principle, in this chapter, we propose to examine the shared memory associated with the study of designing to see how it has grown and matured over time.

What does shared memory contain, in broad terms? The shared memory of an artifact is the collection of all knowledge and its multiple representations that relate to a particular artifact. The four interrelated components of the information contained in the shared memory of the artifact are who, what, how, and why.

Immediately, we run into trouble because it is not always possible to know beforehand what you are going to design. Much like a journalist who roams the streets looking for a story, designers are not always able to know what story they will end up with.

When designing, you start by trying to find a room in that nebulous mind-space, and slowly you arrange that room to accommodate clearer visions and ideas. Then those ideas collide with others, and some emerge unscathed and somewhat sure. The confluence of these ideas is shaped by constraints of budgets, timelines, and attitudes.

Having gone through this process, is it then possible to elicit and elucidate what happened in between? Can we build a codified corpus of knowledge, techniques, and models—the who, what, how, why? The answer is yes because without this shared memory, we would not be able to communicate ideas on designing.

At the same time, it helps to remember that shared memory is an evolving entity. It is shaped by the artifact and shapes the artifact itself.

Thus, we can look at the associated shared memory of the European Union's laws and build a narrative of how the laws governing competition between member states were designed. You can look at the shared memory of a particular make of car and understand why certain safety procedures

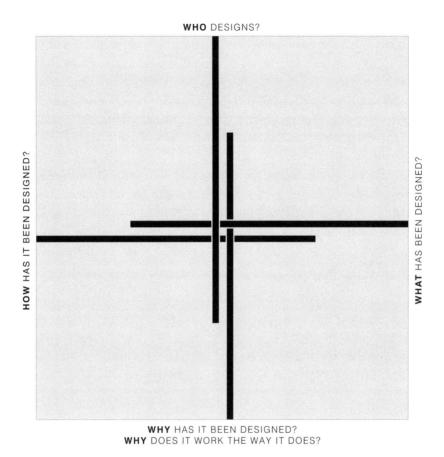

WHO DESIGNS?

HOW HAS IT BEEN DESIGNED?

WHAT HAS BEEN DESIGNED?

WHY HAS IT BEEN DESIGNED?
WHY DOES IT WORK THE WAY IT DOES?

Figure 2.1
The shared memory of the artifact.

have been put in place. Thus, by examining shared memory, you can understand what was designed—the artifact.

Designing and the Shared Memory of the Artifact

The shared memory of the artifact is different from the shared memory
of designing. It is the difference between writing an essay on the weather
and learning to construct a persuasive argument. If you have to write an
essay on the weather, you would learn about the weather—how it changes,
how it is monitored, whether that process is reliable, and which website

provides the most accurate predictions. On the other hand, through this process you would have gained insights into how to persuade someone about your argument, your point of view. If you understand how to construct a persuasive argument, you can use that insight not only to write another essay but also to give speeches, convince your partner to see the movie you want, and make sure your constituency votes for you. The study of designing is thus like understanding how to construct a persuasive argument.

To take another example, the difference between the shared memory of an artifact and shared memory of designing is the difference between studying the city and studying the House of Nine Muses itself. If you wish to understand the city, you would browse the corridors of the House of Nine Muses. What would you do if you wish to study the design of the House of Nine Muses?

You will need records related to it—how it was conceived, who was included in its conception, what its catalogues were over the years, who it was curated by, what their thoughts were, how they debated, what they argued over, how other houses were created and maintained, and how they grew.

Shared memory of the city (artifact)	IS	Contained in the House of Nine Muses
Shared memory of museums	IS	Records and other information related to the design and development of different museums (including the House of Nine Muses) that record a city's lifetime and the people who were involved in these Houses

Similarly, the study of designing is not just about architecture, chairs, or human-computer interaction. It is about all of these and something more— the underlying act that informs and shapes all these different endeavors. This act is the journey from the known to the unknown that is common to an engineer as well as a policymaker, the creation of new knowledge and ideas that both architects and teachers have to contend with, the thread that runs through a carpenter mulling over the needs of her client and a diplomat focused on strategy. It is about drawing from all these diverse fields to understand a very human act, an endeavor that places humans at the center—designing.

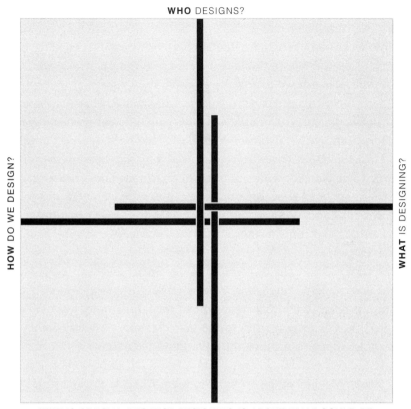

WHO DESIGNS?

HOW DO WE DESIGN?

WHAT IS DESIGNING?

WHY IS CRUCIAL BECAUSE DESIGNING IS ABOUT WHAT COULD BE

Figure 2.2
The shared memory of designing.

Our approach to this chapter is summed up as this:

Understanding (designing) = Examining (shared memory of designing)

What differentiates the study of designing from the study of the natural world lies in the why. In nature, something just is. There is no question of what could be. Designing is about the unborn future and shaping it. Therefore, the why and the who of designing become crucial.

Moreover, the study of designing would remain a how-to manual were it not for insights into the why. Insights into that why are the reason designing can now aspire to the status of a discipline, a step that comes after laying out methods, methodologies, and theories. This chapter traces the journey of design's maturity.

By focusing on shared memory, we use knowledge as the lens with which we choose different events from history. How have different kinds of knowledge been brought together (or not) to understand designing, how has that knowledge been codified, who has access to that knowledge, and what principles are used to organize available knowledge?

The components of shared memory of designing (what is designing, how do we design, who designs and why?) are different from the shared memory of the artifact (who designed it, what has been designed, how has it been designed, why was it designed, and why does it work the way it does?). These differences arise because the shared memory of an artifact is the collection of all knowledge and its multiple representations that relate to a particular artifact. Shared memory of designing places designing as the focal artifact, and consequently, it is all the knowledge available about the act of designing.

We start with the shared memory of the artifact and then move on to the shared memory of designing. When we mention shared memory in this chapter, it refers to the shared memory of the inquiry into designing and its practice. Wherever it refers to the shared memory associated with an artifact, we explicitly mention the artifact associated with it.

The Shared Memory of the Artifact: From the Wheel to the Industrial Revolution

In this section, we cover the history of different artifacts by focusing on what comprised the shared memory of the artifact at that point in time. Let us start with the wheel, which made an appearance in the fourth millennium BC across a broad area extending from the Tigris River to the Rhine River.[3] At that time, if you wanted to know how a wheel was made, you could approach people in the community (provided you could understand them). But that explanation would be incomplete. For instance, if people told you about an apparatus that could help you eat rice off a plate, they could mean a spoon or chop sticks, depending on where you were. It takes a certain development of language to be able to communicate without having the artifact to point to. Thus, the shared memory of the artifact—the wheel, in this case—was contained within the community and the artifact.

The shared memory associated with the wheel, as with the spoon and chopsticks, is very much rooted in the context where it is created, invoked and used. For instance, George Basalla, a historian of technology, points out in his book *Evolution of Technology* that although Mesoamerica's inhabitants knew about the wheel (they created clay figurines that had wheels for mobility), they never used it for transport.[4] The terrain they inhabited was very rugged, and they had ample animal power at their disposal—the context of the object in question. Thus, the understanding of the wheel in Mesoamerica was different from what it was in, say, Europe, and these differences would be reflected in the shared memory of its people.

Context is crucial when it comes to designing. Even if two groups are given the same task, they will end up designing differently because their designs will depend on who they are, where they are from, what they are thinking at that point in time, and their frame of mind, among other things. Context is a nebulous entity that involves both the immediate surroundings as well as the wider socioeconomic and political setting. And so whenever there is an attempt to describe the process of designing, it has to address the specific context along with general descriptions. This has implications for shared memory, too. It always has to account for and accommodate the context in which it has been invoked.

When the wheel was created, people had not developed insights into why the wheel worked the way it did. Thus, the shared memory of the artifact predominantly consisted of knowing the what and how.

Alongside tools, another important aspect of the material culture in ancient times was the design of living spaces—architecture. We draw on this field to understand the next step in the evolution of shared memory—the effect of written language.

Writing allowed shared memory to move beyond the community in time and space. Thus, the insights gained into designing by Marcus Vitruvius Pollio in the first century BC are available to us today at a click of a button because his thoughts were written in a text called *The Ten Books on Architecture* (*De Architectura libri decem*).[5] This text is instructive in understanding how knowing the what and how was conceived in ancient Rome. According to Vitruvius,

> 1. The architect should be equipped with knowledge of many branches of study and varied kinds of learning, for it is by his judgement that all work done by the other arts is put to test. This knowledge is the child of practice and theory. Practice is the continuous and regular exercise of employment where manual work is done with any necessary material according to the design of a drawing. Theory,

on the other hand, is the ability to demonstrate and explain the productions of dexterity on the principles of proportion.

2. It follows, therefore, that architects who have aimed at acquiring manual skill without scholarship have never been able to reach a position of authority to correspond to their pains, while those who relied only upon theories and scholarship were obviously hunting the shadow, not the substance. But those who have a thorough knowledge of both, like men armed at all points, have the sooner attained their object and carried authority with them.[6]

Vitruvius's concerns spanned different fields of study ("The architect should be equipped with knowledge of many branches of study and varied kinds of learning"). What this implies for the how of designing is this: different knowledge bases, all of which are important, have to be synthesized to strive toward a rich design. Thus, the shared memory of the artifact was a crucible where different streams of how commingled to achieve a common objective. It was not a time of specialists because each field had not evolved enough to merit someone who could focus only on one domain. In other words, the who of the shared memory—the designer as conceived back then—is not a specialist but an advanced generalist.

The words of Leonardo da Vinci, the Renaissance savant, echo Vitruvius's philosophy. Writing about Leonardo's views, the editors of *Artists on Art* say, "For him art and science were two closely related activities, two means for describing the physical world": "The mind of the painter," he wrote, "should be like a mirror which is filled with as many images as there are things placed before him."[7]

As the complexity of the objects designed grew, labor had to be divided, leading to a split between the designer and the practitioner. Constructing cathedrals, bridges, temples, and other such grand structures required members of a team to work together under a master. This meant understanding designing as a social process, which in turn meant grappling with shared meaning.

The Renaissance artists created plans, drawings, and sketches to embody this shared meaning they hoped to foster. Here we encounter sketches and drawings—the embodiments of thought and of works in progress, a meta language that captures meanings and connotations that words are inadequate to express. (See chapter 4 for the role played by sketches in the designing process.) For instance, Yves Deforge, a French design scholar, writes in his paper "Avatars of Design: Design before Design" that

Renaissance engineers produced innumerable "theaters of machinery," whose use was related to hydraulics. These ingenious machines could not be built as the technical means to make the parts and transfer the motion—the action of gears and endless screws—to the parts was lacking. ... the design (intention) of Renaissance designers was not to define realizable machines, but rather to illustrate utopias that could eventually be realized (flying, submarine travel, dominating and exploiting the forces of nature) and to give them all the signs of the impressive.[8]

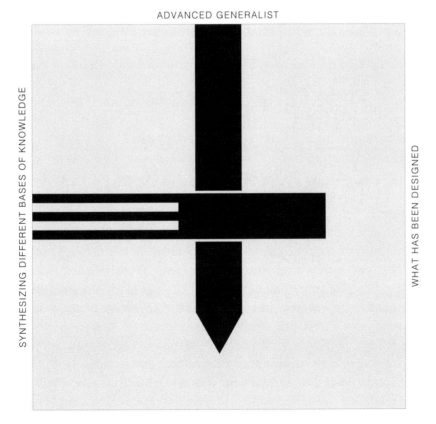

Figure 2.3
How Vitruvius shaped the shared memory of the artifact.

Thus, the shared memory of the artifact acquired a rich visual language of sketches and drawings with a vocabulary that included constructs such as linear perspective. Externalizing ideas in this manner aided communication. This development translated into the slow replacement of the advanced generalist by a team drawn from different fields, where each field has its own shared memory of its community of practice[9] and communicates through the shared meaning embodied in the shared memory of the artifact. The who of the shared memory thus was in these communities of practice.

Ironically, the ability to share across a wider spectrum engendered secrecy, too. The Italian architect Filippo Brunelleschi[10] wanted no one else to understand how he had conceived the design of the dome for the Santa Maria del Fiore cathedral. And so he drew up different plans and split the work among many so that no one could piece all of them together.

Brunelleschi's strategy gives us insight into an obvious yet often ignored feature of the shared memory. It is not as if this accumulated body of knowing what and how was available to all. The social context—the institutions, politics, power structures, and cultural mores—is crucial in determining who can use the shared memory and how they use it. Although knowledge may be inherently secular, the road to access is gated.

In the eighteenth century, some of these gates were demolished, paving the way for the Industrial Revolution, according to historian Joel Mokyr in his book *The Gifts of Athena: Historical Origins of the Knowledge Economy*.[11]

Before the Industrial Revolution, the shared memory of the artifact was transmitted through two modes—parent to child and master to apprentice. "Such a system worked well when the competence to operate a best-practice technique was relatively limited and did not change much between generations and there were few gains from applying knowledge of one field to another," says Mokyr.[12] He describes these times as the "days of engineering without mechanics, iron making without metallurgy, farming without organic chemistry, and medical practice without microbiology."[13]

In other words, people knew what to make and how to make it without understanding why it worked. Mokyr gives the example of winemaking to illustrate his viewpoint: "If manufacturers did not know the nature of fermentation that made sugar into alcohol, they could make wine but without the ability to perfect their flavor or mass-produce at low prices."[14] Without

COMMUNITY OF PRACTICE

Figure 2.4
How communities of practice shaped the shared memory of the artifact.

the why, "it was difficult for technological progress to lead to continued and sustainable improvements," he says.

What happened to make the society curious about knowing the why? Mokyr attributes it to two phenomena—the scientific revolution of the seventeenth century and what he terms as the "Industrial Enlightenment."

During the scientific revolution, empiricism supplanted notions of authority, and the idea took root that nature and the artificial world were governed by the same laws that could be understood, measured, and harnessed. "Scientific method, scientific mentality, and scientific culture set the stage for the Industrial Enlightenment," says Mokyr.[15]

It was during the Industrial Enlightenment that artisanal practices were surveyed and catalogued to determine which techniques were superior and suitable to propagate. The why of these techniques was also examined, and thus these techniques were tamed by understanding the "finite set of principles" that governed them. During this time, there was cooperation and sharing between those who knew the what and how and those who understood the why—"those who knew things and those who made them."[16] The who of the shared memory of designing became a meeting ground for those who knew the how and the why.

Thus, the Industrial Enlightenment paved the road to the Industrial Revolution, and the shared memory of the artifact (which thus far was concerned mainly with knowing the what and the how) acquired the knowledge of the why. The barriers to access were demolished, and a wider emphasis on the why led to a deeper understanding and an explosion in the what. In one way, the Industrial Revolution could be seen as the shared memory of the artifact achieving a certain fullness, with the why commingling with the how and the what.

This maturity of the shared memory also meant that different fields of inquiry started assuming the character of disciplines. The humanities were separated as being a different field of study altogether. The shared memory of the artifact drew from different disciplines, each plumbing the depths of its own inquiry, each with its newly generated language and disciplinary culture.[17]

Slowly, no one person held the shared memory of the artifact. Each person was a specialist in a particular discipline. The age of the Renaissance master who had an overview of all parts of the shared memory of the artifact was over.

Following the Industrial Revolution, complexity continued to increase in terms of both machinery and scale. An increase in complexity meant increasing specialization as the different disciplines in the shared memory of designing continued to forge independent paths. Increased complexity also meant more division of labor.[18] To propagate the shared memory across people working on an assembly line meant making some parts of the shared memory standardized so that it could be transmitted easily.

long note

Figure 2.5
How the Industrial Revolution and its aftermath shaped the shared memory of the artifact.

The Birth of the Shared Memory of Designing

The idea of making underwent a transformation during the Industrial Revolution, given the sheer scale at which production could be possible. Many
histories of design start at this point because this is when the act of making,
the act of design, became a site of study and understanding. We consider
the Industrial Revolution and its aftermath as the transition period from
the shared memory of the artifact to the shared memory of designing. In
the next section, we see how the revolution prompted different people to
respond to it in various ways to articulate what the act of designing should
be named and how it should be studied, organized, archived, and understood. As mentioned earlier, our lens is that of shared memory, which in
turn makes our focus on the knowledge surrounding designing—who holds
the knowledge, who has access to it, and what principles are used to organize the knowledge. We first go through the history chronologically, and
then as we near our times, we try to summarize different approaches that
exist today to understand designing.

The Shared Memory of Designing

John Ruskin, a critic, and William Morris, a designer, turned to crafts
as an alternative to industrial mass production[19] in England. The British
Arts and Crafts movement formed around Morris and was a rally against
the "aesthetic of the machine" that was linked to a certain mode of
production.[20]

If Ruskin and Morris looked toward the past for inspiration in England,
in the Netherlands, a futuristic social and aesthetic utopia was being conceived by the De Stijl group formed in 1917[21]. The important names associated with this group were Theo van Doesburg, Piet Mondrian, and Gerrit T.
Rietveld. The "know why" that drew on a futuristic social and aesthetic utopia translated into a "know how" that adhered to a reductionist aesthetic.
This aesthetic was "characterized in the two-dimensional space by circles,
squares, and triangles and in the three-dimensional space by spheres, cubes,
and pyramids."[22]

By articulating these ideas, what did Morris and the De Stijl group
achieve? They expanded the know why of the artifact to include knowledge
not only of technology but also of society and other considerations that are
relevant to designing. They built a vocabulary to move out of the language

of technology and machines, which is concerned (quite necessarily) with speed and efficiency, and discussed intangible concepts such as quality, aesthetics, and values. Such concepts are the unpolished building blocks of a nascent shared memory of designing.

The Cookbook and the Compass

Let us for a moment examine the nature of these ideas of Morris and De Stijl. Imagine a discussion in an online writers' forum on what the rules are for a monthly competition. What should the brief be like? Should it be detailed (a science-fiction short story based on a doomed love theme within 2,000 words), or should it be more open-ended (a short story on love). It is the difference between a cookbook and a compass. The ideas of Morris and De Stijl do not provide a detailed recipe to design this or that artifact. Rather, they act like a compass, providing overall guidance on which way to turn while designing any artifact.

This tension between whether you provide a cookbook or a compass recurs often in designing. Compared to a compass, a cookbook has less room for exploring alternative paths. It is the same tension between mass production and standardization on one hand and artistic individuality on the other. It was what the German Werkbund—a society of artists, craftsmen, industrialists, and journalists, founded in Munich in 1907 with the goal of improving mass produced goods—lived with.[23] The roots of Bauhaus, the well-known and influential school of design, can be traced back to the German Werkbund. One of the key figures in the Werkbund, Henry van de Velde, formed the Grand Ducal School of Arts and Crafts in Weimar, which later merged with the Academy of Arts in 1919 to form the Bauhaus art school in Weimar.[24]

The Bauhaus and Its Branches

Walter Gropius, the German founder of the Bauhaus, wrote describing the idea of Bauhaus:

> Thus the Bauhaus was inaugurated in 1919 with the specific objective of realizing a modern techtonic art, which like human nature was meant to be all-embracing in its scope. It deliberately concentrated primarily on what has now become a work of imperative urgency—averting mankind's enslavement by the machine by saving the mass-product and the home from mechanical anarchy and by restoring them to purpose, sense and life. This means evolving goods and buildings

specifically designed for industrial production. Our object was to eliminate the drawbacks of the machine without sacrificing any of its real advantages. We aimed at realizing standards of excellence, not creating transient novelties. Experiment once more became the center of architecture, and that demands a broad, coordinating mind, not the narrow specialist.

What the Bauhaus preached was the common citizenship of all forms of creative work, and their logical interdependence on one another in the modern world. Our guiding principle was that design is neither an intellectual or a material affair but simply an integral part of the stuff of life, necessary for everyone in a civilized society.[25]

By calling for "purpose, sense and life," Gropius articulates the why as a future of the material world that is not just about efficiency but that complements efficiency with a sense of what it means to be human.

By outlining a "modern techtonic art," Gropius gave shape to an idea of design that was not tied to a particular artifact but was a study that was "all-embracing in its scope." Like a lighthouse showing the way, it could direct studies of both products and buildings. There was a thread binding them (the "common citizenship of all forms of creative work"), and in conceptualizing design in this fashion, the Bauhaus gave an outline to the what of the shared memory of designing.

What about the how? In 1919, the slogan of Bauhaus was "Art and craft: A new unity," but in 1923, Gropius changed the slogan to "Art and technology: A new unity."[26] These slogans give insights to how the Bauhaus hoped to give body and shape to this common citizenship of all creative forms. Gropius appointed artists such as Wassily Kandinsky, Paul Klee, and László Moholy-Nagy as teachers. The foundation course of the Bauhaus, introduced in 1919–20 by Johannes Itten, was at the core of imparting the how. It was an approach where students experimented and learned and through that learning formed a generalized theory of design.[27]

Although the Bauhaus took the first step in calling for design to be granted the status of a formal discipline, it did not walk down that path. Richard Buchanan writes in his paper "Rhetoric, Humanism and Design" that "When Gropius spoke of the 'comprehensive training' of the new artist, it was more an expression of optimism about future possibilities than accurate reporting about the reality of the Bauhaus program."[28]

After the Bauhaus closed in 1933, it was reborn in 1937 as the New Bauhaus in Chicago. Moholy-Nagy, a fiery Bauhausian, aimed to create a program that would instill a heightened sense of social responsibility in

Figure 2.6
How the Bauhaus shaped the shared memory of designing.

students. In his words, "The coming of an 'electronic age' brings the stringencies of the profit system into even greater conflict with the potentialities such an age has for richer sociobiological economy. … The need for this coordination makes even more pertinent than ever the social obligations of a designer."[29]

In addition to the art and technology that the Bauhaus had drawn from, Moholy-Nagy added a third component to the curriculum he created—science. It was as though the tentative circle Gropius had drawn uniting art and technology was both expanded and made concrete by including science. The shared memory of designing now was the sandbox where art, science, and technology came together.[30] Nagy's attempt was cut short because of financial difficulties.[31]

Meanwhile, other people had joined this quest to braid science, art, and technology into the shared memory of designing: "The mainspring of all our curiosity, or reading, and our theoretical work was our determination to find a solid methodological basis for the work of design. This was a highly ambitious undertaking, admittedly: we were seeking to force through, in the field of design, a transformation equivalent to the process by which chemistry emerged from alchemy."[32] These are the words of Tomas Maldonado, who headed HfG Ulm, a school established by Max Bill and others in 1953 in Germany and which was based on the ideas of Bauhaus. Tomas Maldonado had been Bill's successor.

Ulm focused on the relation between design, science, and technology. The disciplines Ulm drew from included ergonomics, mathematical techniques, economics, physics, politics, psychology, semiotics, and sociology.[33] Mathematical disciplines including combinatorial analysis and topology were brought in to explore possible applications to design. In other words, the attempt was to articulate and legitimize designing by framing a methodology that drew from science and mathematics. How far did this articulation go?

Richard Buchanan, author and design scholar, says: "Ulm should not be credited with initiating the 'design methods movement' or the effort to find a neo-positivist science of design thinking." He goes on to say that it was more of a "meeting ground" for people with such interests.[34] And Bernhard E. Bürdek says in the section about "The Educational Impact of the Ulm School of Design" in his book *Design: History, Theory and Practice of Product Design* that "The field of design methodology, in particular, would be unimaginable without the work of the Ulm School of Design."[35]

Whether or not the design methods movement began at Ulm or was nourished by it in the late 1950s and the early 1960s, the vocabulary of design was inspired heavily by science. Terms like *rational, functional, deterministic, solution oriented,* and *efficient* became part of the vocabulary of designing.

The Elusive Quest for a Traditional Science of Designing

Before we proceed, let us stop and ponder the question of whether design-ing can be like a traditional science, such as the physical sciences. This is a question that many working on the study of designing grappled with. Can designing be a discipline that can be formally encoded and taught? Can you have a design textbook like you have a textbook for traditional science? It is a tempting idea, for various reasons.

For starters, traditional science does not concern itself with matters of culture, politics, society, and environmental sustainability. In other words, traditional science is context-independent; it is considered universal. Tradi-tional science stands for explanation and predictability. You can calculate beforehand where the car will be if it travels at a certain speed over a certain period of time. Moreover, traditional science enjoys legitimacy. It is under-stood to have a certain system behind it, which provides assurance and certitude. These are but some of the reasons that the search for a science of designing became an attractive idea.

In 1963, Welsh designer John Chris Jones and lecturer on architecture D. G. Thornley organized the first conference on design methods in England. It was the first "scientific approach to design methods in England."[36] Then came the first PhD thesis on design methods.[37] It broke new ground in architecture and was a harbinger of what the author would continue to do again and again—challenge the field with his ideas and contrarian views. Christopher Alexander's "Notes on the Synthesis of Form" contained in a thesis all the motifs and ideas being explored in design methods in his time. The core idea was that of hierarchical decomposition. It was a Cartesian approach: the whole can be split into parts that can be isolated. You then solve individual parts and then combine them to solve the whole.[38]

The Mark of Design: Why?

If you consider the shared memory of designing built by such Cartesian approaches, they do not dwell on the why. Just as gravity is not considered a question that can be voted on, in their approach, design was implicitly legitimate because the traditional science-inspired approach deemed it so.

But the artifacts created by design do not enjoy the implicit legitimacy granted to traditional science. Rather, the difference between designing and

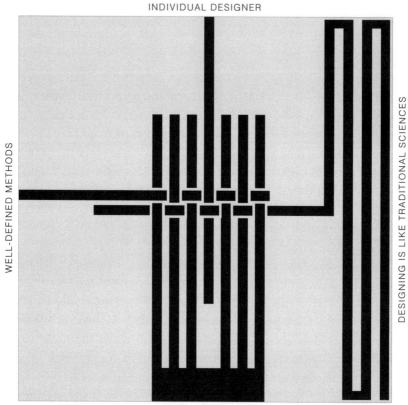

Figure 2.7
How Cartesian approaches shaped the shared memory of designing.

traditional science is that traditional science is about "what is" and designing concerns itself with "what could be." It is about exploring an unknown future. Therefore, why a particular path for the future might be followed is subject to argument, debate, questioning, vote, as well as social, cultural, and political constraints. It is messy, confusing, without clear answers, without certitude. Simply put, designing necessarily has to deal with humans in all their diversity and variety.[39]

This tension between a humanist view of design and a more traditional science-inspired design was articulated by Geoffrey Broadbent, one of the organizers of the 1967 Design Methods in Architecture symposium held in Portsmouth:

> The Symposium had been set up by Tony Ward to include a specific combination between those whom he saw as behaviorists, representing a mechanized, quantified view of design, and those (including himself) he saw as existentialist/phenomenologist (formerly Marxist) concerned, above all, "with humanness" of human beings.[40]

Sciences of the Artificial

Can approaches that work for natural sciences be used for studying the artificial, or do we need a different approach? It was this question that propelled the polymath and Nobel Prize–winner Herbert A. Simon to articulate for the first time in detail the need for a separate discipline to study the human-made—the study of designing.

Simon articulated the pitfalls in using the approaches that worked for natural sciences for problems that relate to "professions with empirical and theoretical substance distinct from the substance of their supporting sciences."[41] He said these professions are all tackling the same beast: they are dealing with a world that is artificial and not natural. He called for a new field of study, the sciences of the artificial, which also was the title of the seminal work he authored in 1969.

He describes his insight into understanding whether artificial phenomena fell within the compass of science:

> Finally, I thought I began to see in the problem of artificiality an explanation of the difficulty that has been experienced in filling engineering and other professions with empirical and theoretical substance distinct from the substance of their supporting sciences. Engineering, medicine, business, architecture, and

painting are concerned not with the necessary but with the contingent—not with how things are but how they might be—in short, with design.[42]

In one leap, he had thrown open the doors of design enquiry to welcome diverse fields, such as medicine, business, law, and education. Making a case that "everyone who devises courses of action aimed at changing existing situations into preferred ones"[43] is a professional designer, Simon says that "design so construed is the core of all professional training; it is the

INDIVIDUAL DESIGNER

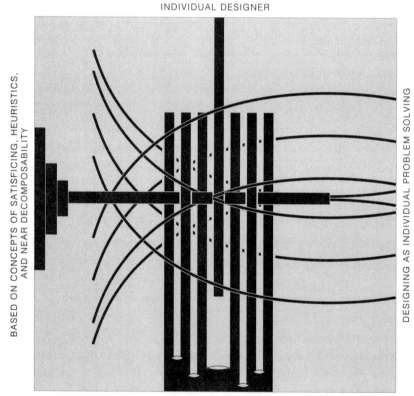

LEGITIMACY DRAWN FROM THE EMERGING FIELDS OF COGNITIVE
SCIENCE AND ARTIFICIAL INTELLIGENCE

Figure 2.8
How Simon's approach shaped the shared memory of designing.

principal mark that distinguishes the professions from the sciences. Schools of engineering, as well as schools of architecture, business, education, law, and medicine, are all centrally concerned with the process of design."[44]

Questioning, then, why engineering schools are reduced to teaching physics and mathematics; medical schools, biological sciences; and business schools, finite mathematics, he says that schools hanker after academic respectability and want a subject matter that is "intellectually tough, analytic, formalizable, and teachable."[45] But so far, the study of design had been "intellectually soft, intuitive, informal, and cookbooky."[46]

Simon's ideas on designing stemmed from theories of individual cognition, which adhered to the "mind as a computing machine" metaphor. If the human mind is a computer, then any activity the mind performs, including designing, can be viewed as problem solving.[47] Simon's view of designing (the what) thus was "designing as problem solving," which drew legitimacy from his theories of individual cognition.

If designing is problem solving, then how does the process unfold? First, designing, according to Simon, is a complex problem, such complex problems require enormous amounts of computing power, and like computers, the human mind also is limited in its capability to find optimal solutions to such complex problems. What then does the human mind do? According to Simon, the human mind does not search for optimal solutions but for satisfactory ones, and he termed this process *satisficing*.

The limited computing power of the human mind thus gives rise to what Simon termed *bounded rationality*, which was against the dominant view in economics at that time. The dominant view in economics then saw human beings as rational beings who make optimal choices in order to maximize utility. According to Simon, constrained by bounded rationality, human beings can only satisfice and not optimize.[48] However, he claimed that the human mind is clever enough that it uses rules of thumb developed from experience, or heuristics, as a way to address the complexity of the problem being solved. Moreover, according to Simon, complex problems involve a lot of interdependencies, which makes it hard to break them into completely independent parts. In order to circumvent this issue, Simon proposed that the decomposition is "nearly decomposable" because the system is partially decomposed while retaining some aspects of the interdependence of the system.[49] Thus, the how of designing, according to Simon, is rooted in the concepts of satisficing, heuristics, and near decomposability.[50]

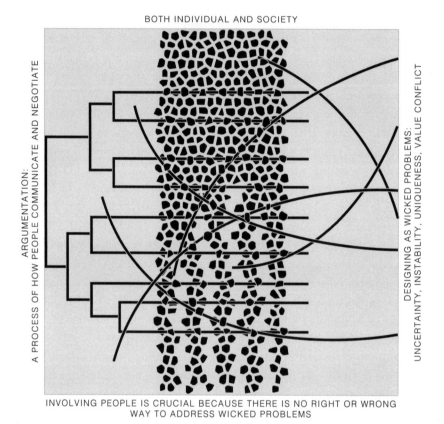

Figure 2.9

How approaches that let go of the Cartesian approach shaped the shared memory of designing.

Letting Go of the Cartesian Approach

All this while, there was an increasing awareness and acknowledgment that a Cartesian approach would not work for designing. In an interview in 1970, architect and prolific author Christopher Alexander repudiated the design methodology being followed:[51]

> I feel that a terrific part of it has become an intellectual game, and it's largely for that reason that I've dissociated from the field. I resigned from the Board of Directors of the DMG Newsletter because I felt that the purpose which the magazine represents is not really valuable, and I don't want to be identified with them. (DMG stands for Design Methods Group.)

Why do problems in designing elude Cartesian approaches? According to design theorists Horst Rittel and Melvin Webber, it is because design problems are "wicked problems." In a 1973 paper mildly titled "Dilemmas in a General Theory of Planning," Rittel and Webber outlined different characteristics of such wicked problems.[52] A wicked problem cannot be clearly defined, it has no stopping rule, there are no true or false solutions to it, and it is connected to many other problems. Design methods that subscribed to a system approach were ill-equipped to solve such problems because they were inherently ill-defined. In order to tackle wicked problems, Rittel said that a new generation of design methods had to be developed. These "second-generation design methods" would establish a continuity, a lineage between the previous methods that took inspiration from science and the methods Rittel proposed rather than letting there be a rupture.[53]

What were these second-generation methods? Rittel's methods started with defining the design problem through argumentation instead of assuming that a clear definition existed beforehand. Werner Kunz and Rittel developed IBIS (Issue-Based Information System) to support argumentation for planning problems.[54] Involving users in the design decisions, such as identifying what the problem is, was at the heart of second-generation methods.

However, can users themselves decide everything, without anyone's intervention? According to Alexander, they can if they know the right language to do so. In his 1977 book, *A Pattern Language: Towns, Buildings, Construction*,[55] he writes that structures, buildings, and objects possess their own language, and using 253 detailed examples, he lays out the individual words or patterns that constitute the vocabulary of this language. They can be stitched together to form infinite combinations, just as we do with language itself. New experiences and observations can create new patterns, so they are not rigid but can be evolved further. Using these patterns, you could build regions, cities, neighborhoods, even seating, colors, and lighting.[56]

If Alexander's way was to say that the users could design for themselves, Donald A. Schön in his 1983 book *The Reflective Practitioner: How Professionals Think in Action* moved away from the Cartesian approach by describing what he termed "reflection-in-action."[57] Schön starts with trying to understand the epistemology of practice and examines how similar or different it is from the kind of knowledge valued in academia. He characterizes practice to include "complexity, uncertainty, instability, uniqueness, and value conflict" and argues that "technical rationality," the dominant paradigm then, is inadequate to address the needs of practice.[58] Technical rationality sees professional activity as "instrumental problem solving made rigorous by application of scientific theory and technique."[59] Given its focus on problem solving, technical rationality did not focus on "problem setting," which Schön says is central to practice. He describes problem setting as "a process in which, interactively, we *name* the things to which we will attend and *frame* the context in which we will attend to them."[60]

Instead of separating practice as application of knowledge, as technical rationality claimed it was, Schön called for recognizing the knowledge inherent in practice, the knowledge that evolved along with practice that enriched practice in turn. He termed the process "reflection-in-action": "It is this entire process of reflection-in-action which is central to the 'art' by which practitioners sometimes deal well with situations of uncertainty, instability, uniqueness, and value conflict."[61]

Different Models of Designing

Now that we are nearing times closer to our own, we have a multitude of languages to use to talk about designing. It is as though each of us is looking at a different House of Nine Muses and trying to explain in his or her own way how it came into being. Some of us focus on the houses themselves, some focus on the process by which how they were created, some try to talk about how people have argued about them.

There are different categorizations of the different design methods, methodologies, and theories. Instead of separating out theories, methods, and methodologies, we refer to all attempts to understand designing as different models of designing. Because our intent is to explain the idea behind these different models and unpack what are the gaps and strengths, we will not delve into too much detail in explaining the models themselves. We have references everywhere for those readers who are keen to dive deeper.

The measure we have chosen to categorize different contemporary models of designing is that of messiness. Designing, as we have seen thus far, is a messy affair that involves a diverse set of people, disciplines, artifacts, and contexts, and there has been a constant effort to tame or contend with that messiness. Different models of designing tackle this messiness to varying degrees. Based on how much messiness these models embrace, we have divided contemporary models on designing into the following categories—nonmessy, slightly messy, more messy, more-the-messier, and most messy models.

Nonmessy Models

Nonmessy models of designing view designing problems as closer to problems in the traditional sciences, similar to the first-generation methods described by Rittel. The why of these models of designing relies on the legitimacy given to traditional sciences. If such methods and approaches work for traditional sciences, then they will work for designing, too.

These models of designing rely on a certain amount of clarity in the what or how of designing. They offer a prescriptive how: the process of designing is linear with well-defined and clearly articulated steps, and in some cases, these models assume that the what that needs to be designed is also well-known. There is no who explicitly stated in such models.

Examples of nonmessy models A popular approach found in different engineering design textbooks today, which is an exemplar of such nonmessy models, is by Gerhard Pahl and Wolfgang Beitz.[62]

The approach proposed by Vladimir Hubka and W. Ernst Eder[63] initially focused on engineering design but was subsequently presented as a theory of technical systems and then as design science. Although broader in perspective, it and other prescriptive approaches could be described as follows.

The designing process (the how) is seen as a sequence of activities leading to intermediate results. There are four phases of activities—clarification of the task, conceptual design, embodiment layout, and detail design. As mentioned earlier, it is as if design problems were problems in traditional sciences. The objects to be designed (the what) are technical systems that transform energy, material, and information. The functional behavior of a technical system is fully determined by principles of physics and can be described by laws of physics.

The goal of a design problem is somewhat different from the goals of the physical sciences. Although a design problem seeks to define the geometry and find the materials of the system so that the required and prespecified physical behavior is realized in the most effective and efficient way, the way the problems are set up and the methods employed for solving them are much like those in the physical sciences. Moreover, it is assumed that design should proceed from the abstract to the concrete in order to keep the solution space as large as possible and that complex problems should be split into subproblems for which subsolutions are to be found and synthesized into overall solutions for the design problem.

The other set of nonmessy approaches start from the artifact. They rely on the premise that designing starts with reasonably complete specifications (the nonmessy what) and universal methods purportedly exist (the how), which can then be used to arrive at the artifact. General design theory (GDT) by Hiroyuki Yoshikawa is one such theory.[64] In the ideal case, it is as though you have a catalogue of artifacts with different specifications, and it is a matter of selecting which artifact fits yours. In practice, however, GDT maps the specifications to the artifact through a step-wise process— conjecture, analysis, and evaluation of design.[65]

Slightly Messy Models

But unlike the natural sciences, as we describe earlier, designing has to deal with the messiness of people, culture, politics, and society. It is usually not possible to have clarity on either the process (the how) or the artifact (the what) beforehand. For instance, would you call the sketches you make while thinking about what kind of kitchen you want to create an artifact? Or would you call the blueprints an artifact?

The first level of messiness is introduced by acknowledging that the artifact and process are not clearly defined entities; both are affected by each other continuously. Therefore, some messiness is introduced by how the idea was approached—by taking the linear model and replacing it with a spiral structure (the how) that emphasized preconceptions at different stages.[66]

Examples of Slightly Messy Models   A hybrid model of designing was developed by Nigel Cross, a British design researcher.[67] At all levels, a dependency between the problem and the solution is identified. The hybrid model also recognizes the necessity of building an overall solution from subsolutions by generating, combining, evaluating, and choosing appropriate subsolutions.

Enter the Individual: More Messy Models

As more empirical studies of designing started being done, the need to acknowledge messiness in designing strengthened. When individual designers were observed in the process of designing, the knowledge that emerged from practice spurred the creation of models of designing that acknowledge the individual in different ways.

Examples of More Messy Models of Designing That Acknowledge the Individual   Herbert A. Simon's approach (described earlier in the chapter) acknowledges the individual by bringing in individual cognition into understanding designing. Simon's approach is tricky for our classification. Although he acknowledges the individual designer and the attendant messiness, he circumvents the messiness introduced by the who with the how. He models the how as individual problem solving, which is similar to the how proposed in the nonmessy models of designing.

Donald Schön brought into focus individual designers (the who) at work and modeled the designing process as a self-reflective act (the how). Schön's case studies try to understand the practice of designing, and he captures the messiness involved as a conversation between who is working (the designers) and what is being designed. He calls for a self-reflective practitioner who is conscious of the thought process that goes into the act of design and uses that information in other design efforts.

Another theory that is agnostic when it comes to the who is Armand Hatchuel's and Benoit Weil's[68] C-K (concept-knowledge) theory. C-K theory introduces messiness by modeling designing as the process of journeying into the unknown (the how)—for you do not know beforehand what will emerge from the process of designing (the what is not known beforehand). C-K theory fully acknowledges and addresses the point in designing when a new unknown object—a concept—emerges from existing knowledge without logical deduction. Because a similar situation exists in the mathematical technique of forcing, C-K theory uses that mathematical technique as its formal justification.

C-K is therefore the interplay between knowledge whose logical status is known and concepts whose logical status is unknown (the how). The formal foundation allows C-K to make claims about, among other things, the nature of knowledge and its influence on design and on the ways that concepts are developed. It also explains that concept generation and elaboration are unimportant if they do not lead to learning and knowledge expansion.

The Social: More-the-Messier Models

So far, the approaches we have spoken about deal directly with the how and what and a limited who of designing—limited because designing is a social process and the who involves a group of people, not just an individual. If the social aspect of designing is taken into account, the why enters the picture too. Earlier, the why was either implicit, or it was assumed that the how and what would take care of it. But if we are to think of designing as shaping the world around us, constrained by the political, cultural, and societal realities, the why takes center stage. Acknowledging the importance of why, some models characterize the design process as a social act—one where people deliberate, discuss, debate, and try to figure out the why.

Examples of More-the-Messier Models of Designing That Acknowledge the Social Are deliberations and discussions among different people during designing so important that they require our attention and understanding? Louis L. Bucciarelli, a professor of engineering, answers with an emphatic yes. Based on his studies of engineers designing together, he characterizes the process of designing as a social process (the who) that involves negotiations during which designers build different kinds of discourses (the how).[69]

In order to implement C-K (concept-knowledge) theory in practice, a practical method called KCP (knowledge-concept-propositions) was developed, which involves different people with a diverse set of knowledge bases in designing process (the who). The KCP process involves charting the state of the art of K (knowledge), including all products, technologies, and business aspects related to the organization (the how). The second stage involves creating interesting concepts that may lead to disruptive innovations. A major driving force of this generation is available knowledge rather than free brainstorming or similar techniques. The last step involves proposing innovative design strategies that exploit the knowledge and concepts in the best way. The move from C-K theory to the KCP method is a way to bring different people and the knowledge bases they hold into the process of designing, thus accounting for the messiness of the practicalities of designing.

Rittel introduced the idea of argumentation (the how) to bring in the social dimension of designing. For instance, in all the models described above, negotiations take place at every stage. How do these negotiations affect the entire process? How does communication take place? How does sense making occur? These are questions that the people who unearthed the social aspect of designing delved into, providing a much richer idea of designing.

Designing as rhetoric (the how) is another characterization that emphasizes the social nature of design, as conceptualized by Richard Buchanan. In "Rhetoric, Humanism, and Design," he says, "Design has become an art of deliberation essential for making, in all phases of human activity."[70] Making includes in its ambit theories, policies, institutions, manufactured objects, and objects (such as plans, proposals, models, and sketches) used for designing. He describes design thus: "Design is the art of shaping arguments about the artificial or human-made world, arguments which may be carried forward in the concrete activities of production in each of these areas, with objective results ultimately judged by individuals, groups, and society."[71]

Another way of bringing in the social is to look at the intermediate outputs of the designing process—models, sketches, plans, and drawings.[72] These become a trace of the designing process as they capture the social negotiations. Bringing in the social also complicates how cognition is understood, which requires theories of social cognition to be brought into designing.

Enter Context: Most Messy Models

Broadly, context is about weaving together different threads, including the social, political, cultural, and economic elements that are specific to a particular situation at hand. Take the conversations around smartphones in popular media. When there is discussion of design, almost no attention is paid to the conditions in which these phones are produced, the global supply chain, a culture driven by consumption, and the environmental impact.

Context is a messy, hairy affair. It is multidimensional: you can go deep both in breadth and depth of understanding the context. For instance, context could mean understanding whether touchscreens are suited to an environment that is humid and always sunny. It could also mean the ways that touchscreens are becoming markers of aspiration. Context is about the current social, economic, and political climate that fuels the use of smartphones.

Context is about acknowledging diversity and the interconnectedness of these diverse threads. Take disciplinary diversity. In one design of the smartphone, you need to think of language, communication, material attributes, broader social issues, and institutional structures. Context makes you confront the intangible elements that make us human—culture, bias, power systems, subversions. Context brings focus into values: What kind of a society are we designing for? Who is the *we* who participates in the conversation?

The models of design that aim to represent designing in a formal way and focus on the how and what do not deal directly with context. The models that focus on the social allow for a more context-specific design. But there is still a large gap in being able to address context in a multilayered way that allows for diversity in all the models.

So Many Threads

As we have seen, there are different models of how designing is understood, and each model illuminates the process of designing in its unique way. If the focus is on the what and the how and the approach is too formal, albeit theoretically elegant, it may not resonate with practice. Additionally, if the focus is on the what and the how, the approach may not adequately address context and the larger picture involving the cultural and political implications.

If the focus is on the why, the approaches address the social, cultural, and political context but sometimes do not provide adequate insights into how to translate that into practice. Context becomes the focal point when social scientists and philosophers take up design as a subject of their study, but there is not a common vocabulary for them to communicate with and influence the design community and for it to translate into practice. Therefore, we need to conceive designing in a way that both addresses the what, how, and why and resonates with practice.

Second, different areas of study—such as management, public policy, development studies, and urban studies—concern themselves with the act of designing and, given their focus, choose to interpret designing the way it most resembles the act they are trying to understand. Because all these fields recognize the undercurrent of designing that runs through them, designing can play the role of an interlocutor between these different areas of study. But most of the conversations remain in silos because there is no accessible common language for all of them to converse with each other. Therefore, we need to conceive designing in a way that is inherently transdisciplinary.

Third, and most important, we need to place people at the center of designing. We need to conceive of designing in a manner so that the who implies diverse perspectives participating in designing.

These different threads are tangled. It is as though there is a network of tensions that pull them in different directions. The tensions are between theory and practice, the individual and the social, and the contextual and the universal and between the need to address the who, what, how, and why of designing. The idea is to weave them into a coherent quilt. In the next four chapters, we attempt to create that quilt and tell you its story in a new language. It is a language in which we can have a meaningful dialogue about design between theory and practice, across different disciplines, and with context playing a pivotal role.

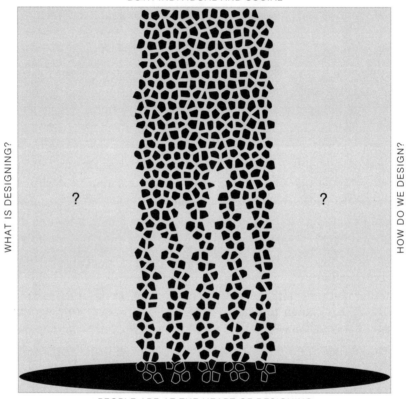

Figure 2.10
The questions that remain about our contribution to the shared memory of designing.

3 We the Designers

Dear, dear! How queer everything is to-day! And yesterday things went on just as usual. I wonder if I've been changed in the night? Let me think: was I the same when I got up this morning? I almost think I can remember feeling a little different. But if I'm not the same, the next question is, Who in the world am I? Ah, THAT'S the great puzzle!

—Lewis Carroll, *Alice's Adventures in Wonderland*

Looking at "a Wave"

We start by resting awhile with Mr. Palomar on the sandy shores of a beach where he has chosen to take a vacation. Let us watch him. The Italian author Italo Calvino wrote about Mr. Palomar's musings in an eponymous book, and in our first encounter, Mr. Palomar is preoccupied with a seemingly simple task—looking at a wave.[1] Mr. Palomar is specific: he wants to look at "a wave." But as Calvino informs us, it is a trickier problem than what Mr. Palomar originally thought it would be:

> But it is very difficult to isolate one wave, separating it from the wave immediately following it, which seems to push it and at times overtakes it and sweeps it away; just as it is difficult to separate that one wave from the wave that precedes it and seems to drag it towards the shore, unless it turns against its follower as if to arrest it. Then, if you consider the breadth of the wave, parallel to the shore, it is hard to decide where the advancing front extends regularly and where it is separated and segmented into independent waves, distinguished by their speed, shape, force, direction. In other words, you cannot observe a wave without bearing in mind the complex features that concur in shaping it and the other, equally complex ones that the wave itself originates.[2]

In the previous chapter, we presented different approaches to under-standing designing, all of which were trying to comprehend the elusive wave that is designing. Some, using design theorist Horst Rittel's first-generation methods, have tried pinning it down by defining it clearly, akin to marking a boundary and calling that a wave. And just as you cannot define a wave by marking its boundaries, these methods found that in prac-tice such definitions were not functional. Other theorists tried to loosen the definition, but they too found themselves struggling.

In this chapter, we outline our attempt to understand designing, which is somewhat like understanding the composition of a fugitive entity like a wave. Let's again listen to Calvino, who tells us Mr. Palomar's thoughts:

> So, to understand the composition of a wave, you have to consider these oppos-ing thrusts, which are to some extent counterbalanced and to some extent added together, to produce a general shattering of thrusts and counter-thrusts in the usual spreading of foam.[3]

The different approaches we saw earlier either focused on the thrust or counterthrust by navigating different ranges in between. For Simon, it was problem solving. For Rittel, it was argumentation. But it is a bit of both and something more. Focusing on either the thrust or the counterthrust gives us only part of the picture. How do we then try to grasp the whole?

A Game of the Whole and Its Parts

Let us leave Mr. Palomar to his thoughts (that often frustrate him) and turn our attention to two children playing with five brightly colored blocks on the sand, awash with sunlight. One child takes the five cubes and arranges them on top of each other to form a tower. The other child kicks the tower and places three cubes on the ground and two on top of them, making a sort of pyramid. The tower, unlike the wave, is clearly made of those five blocks. The whole is a sum of its constituent parts. A bicycle, for example, has two wheels, a chain, handlebars, and a structure that holds the parts together. We can determine how the bicycle will behave based on the dif-ferent components it is made of and the relationships between them. The behavior is predictable. If we need to construct another bicycle, we can follow the same process by assembling it from its constituent parts. Our approach to understanding the bicycle can be described as follows:

Characteristic	The whole can be split into its constituent parts. Each part is clearly defined. The relationship between the parts is fixed.
Behavior	Its behavior is predictable. It can be determined using knowledge of the parts.

Such an approach is Cartesian (after the French mathematician René Descartes). It is based on the principle of reduction (the whole can be separated into parts) and the principle of disjunction (each part can be defined fully, and the relationship between different parts is fixed).[4] If the entire universe adhered to these principles, it would be possible to predict its behavior exactly, a claim made by Descartes as well.

But to predict what the universe does, the predictor needs to be clearly separate and distinct from the universe. Apply the ideas of Descartes to the entire universe, and separate people from the material environment, which we call nature and which can be said to be an invention of the ancient Greeks:

> The greatest of all Greek scientific discoveries was the discovery—or rather, as philosopher Geoffrey Lloyd put it, the invention—of nature itself. The Greeks defined nature as the universe minus human beings and their culture. Although this seems to us to be the most obvious sort of distinction, no other civilization came upon it.[5]

What are the consequences of such an approach? You can keep dividing a whole into different parts. For instance, you can separate the mind from the body. And then you split the body into different parts and study each part in isolation: the heart is a pump, the kidneys are filters, and arteries are pipes. The body is a machine. Similarly, you can study the mind as an entity unaffected by the body it resides in. The mind as a computer paradigm flows naturally from this approach, which polymath and Nobel Prize–winner Herbert A. Simon subscribed to.

What are the consequences for designing? For starters, this model aspires to a linear process, such as analysis-synthesis or evaluation. Despite the feedback mechanisms integrated into this model, at its heart beats a linear process.

Second, this is a flattening approach to designing. Take a transportation project. If you think of the transportation project as being made of the blocks a child was playing with, then you can identify different components, such as economics, a process to acquire land, the machinery required, and people. Whether the transportation project is for Kathmandu, Kinshasa, or Kyoto, you can execute the same process. It is as though the transportation project is a plug that can be inserted anywhere, and Kathmandu, Kinshasa, and Kyoto are nothing but interchangeable sockets.

Enter Our Protagonist: Context

This is where our orderly idea of the wave runs into a squall because Kathmandu and Kinshasa are anything but obedient blocks. These cities determine context, and their context is different from that of Kyoto. The word *context* does not evoke a fanfare of trumpets, as might befit the entrance of a crucial character in a story. But it should. The word sounds dull, like a forgotten textbook sitting on the fourth shelf of a rarely visited library. But it is anything but dull. It is a word that literally weaves together various elements. Context is formed from Latin word *contextus* (from *con* for "together" and *texere* for "to weave"). But what does it weave together? It helps braid the what, how, who, and why of designing. It is the soil in which the meaning of designing grows. For designing, it is like the air we breathe. Without it, designing would be lifeless.

Why can't context be treated like an obedient building block—a well-oiled part in your complicated machinery or a well-defined part of the whole? The reason is twofold—definition and relationship. When you build public transportation—say, a metro train—for a city, the metro affects the city, and the city is affected by the metro.[6] If context is the situation, the surroundings, the circumstances, and the setting, can you remove the metro from the city and still call that the context, or do both the metro and the city together form the context? How would you define the wave when both the sea and the wave define each other?

Why is context crucial to design? Take the case of a US retail giant that started operations in Germany but had to shut them down. When asked about the failure, its former head said, "We didn't realize pillowcases are a different size in Germany."[7] Although it seems a simple enough idea—that we should pay more attention to context—we seem to be taken by surprise when the one-size-fits-all approach fails.

Take the case of a development project in a village in a state in east India.[8] The government decided to intervene with a dairy development scheme that aimed to improve the villagers' livelihoods, despite the village being in a milk-surplus district. Some farmers were given cows impregnated with imported semen of a high-yielding breed. The local bulls were subjected to a major castration drive so that the high-yielding cows did not mate with these bulls. Some farmers were asked to grow a specific species of tree that could become the fodder for all these cows. Two years and twenty million rupees (about $280,000) later, the project saw eight cross-bred calves and not a single tree. Important questions (such as why start a dairy development project in a milk-surplus district or why plant a species of trees most unsuited to its land) were never asked. In other words, the people who were the intended beneficiaries of the scheme were never consulted about the plan's goals and methods.[9]

Context is about people. If context is about weaving together various elements, every thread is connected to people, their families, and their mores, traditions, needs, customs, culture, desires, fights, and biases. Is it possible to reduce these to neat variables that can be assigned a convenient value? Can questions about people (what motivates people, what pleases them aesthetically, what do they value, what do they ignore, what makes them afraid?) be transformed into plug-and-play answers that can fit into any problem? Many variables—the intricacies of the government bodies people have erected, the attitudes of the people responsible for those bodies, the nature of the power structures within them—affect people and, in turn, the things that are being designed for them.

Context is messy, but designing cannot survive without context. It is about situating living beings at the center. The blocks can be arranged in a tower, but when you bring in those children, you have a different situation altogether. Their actions—how those children interact with the blocks, what meanings they make out of them, and how they arrange them, play with them, and design with them—decide the final outcome. Those children, along with what they like and what they wish to create, are intangibles that are part of the context.

A gun is made of different parts, but designing a gun is not just about those parts. It is also about the person who is going to handle the gun. The reason the gun is going to be used, the meaning of having a gun inside a home, and the laws that govern guns and the people using them are all encompassed in that one word—context. Understanding living beings, the social groups they belong to, and their institutional structures and power relationships implies understanding context. Any theory of designing without this context remains an empty shell that is not infused with life.

Thinking of Monkeys

If we want to arrive at a conception of designing that can give context its due importance, how do we proceed? One approach is to go the opposite way: instead of a linear process, let us think of a nonlinear process. Instead of objects that are defined and stable with clearly marked relationships, let us go to a world that is unstable and does not have well-defined objects or stable relationships.

By adopting this opposite path, we are now in negative space. In art, negative space is the space that surrounds the subject of the artwork. It becomes as important as the subject itself because the negative space lends definition to the subject. In some cases, this negative space is used quite cleverly. Think about the FedEx logo, for instance, where an arrow is formed by the negative space between the letters *e* and *x*. Even if we focus on the negative space, we remain within the same frame. As George Lakoff,[10] the cognitive linguist would say, "We are not thinking differently." What does he mean?

To understand this, let's read about the folktale of a king who suffered from a tummy ache. The medicine wizard prescribed a tonic made of exotic herbs and told the king that the tonic would solve his ailment but only on one condition: he should not think of monkeys while taking the medicine. The king went home. When it was time to take the medicine, all he could think of was a monkey. The shadow of a fern reminded him of a furry tail. A cackle outside was the chatter of simians. When his child came running to him with her supper smeared on her face, all he could think was "such a dear chimp." Thus the medicine wizard's counsel proved to have the exact opposite effect of the king because it did not change the frame of the king's thoughts.

In his book *Don't Think of an Elephant! Know Your Values and Frame the Debate: The Essential Guide for Progressives*,[11] Lakoff talks about how we have a network of associations attached to different words. An elephant evokes associations of huge animals, trunks, and circuses. He calls this set of associations a "frame." By using language such as "unstable," "nonlinear," and other such negatives, we continue to dwell in the same frame as before.

When the frame is changed, it alters how we view the world. An illustration of this comes from India, where the brutal rape of a young woman in a bus moving through the streets of the capital led to a widespread debate on how laws related to sexual assault should be reformed. A commission was appointed under J. S. Verma,[12] a former judge of the Supreme Court of India. This commission's report changed the frame of the system. Instead of "women's safety" as the centerpiece, the commission's report chose "women's autonomy." All the previous concerns regarding women's safety remain intact. For instance, a patriarchal way of ensuring women's safety would be to ask them to stay at home after dark. But this response would not hold if the anchor is women's autonomy. The system would then have to provide ways of ensuring the safety of women while respecting their freedom. Similarly, can we conceive of this alternative view of designing? Can we change the frame?

Context and Complex: Two Sides of the Same Coin

The words *context* and *complex* have similar roots. The word *context*, as was shown earlier, means "to weave together." *Complex* also has its roots in *com* ("together") and *plectere* ("weave"). What if we view designing, where context is crucial, as a complex system? In 1984, at the Santa Fe Institute, the term *complex system* was used to describe dynamical systems with a large number of interactions and feedback, inside of which processes very difficult to predict and control take place.[13] Whether ant colonies, economies, stock markets, or the World Wide Web, these systems produce and use information and signals from both their internal and external environments and, in doing so, learn and adapt. These systems have innumerable components that produce characteristics such as complex, hard-to-predict, and changing patterns of behavior. There is no clear definition of a complex adaptive system, but these are the different characteristics that mark them.[14] Can we conceive of designing as a study of a complex adaptive system? What would such a conception be?

A Game of Whole and Parts Revisited

Let us return to the beach. How do we understand a wave? We said we look at how the thrusts and counterthrusts interact with each other. The definition of a wave is elusive, but we can try to understand how these thrusts and counterthrusts interact, how these *processes* shape the wave. This gives us a clue as to how to proceed. From defining objects, we try to understand processes. From nouns or objects, we focus now on verbs or processes.

What were the different nouns that we used in chapter 2 during our discussions on different approaches to designing? We wondered whether to focus on the individual or the social and whether to conceive of a descriptive approach or a prescriptive approach. When the whole is split into parts, we need to focus on the parts and the objects and choose between one or the other. What if we conceive of a different whole that is shaped constantly by what constitutes it? Like a group of waves that together cause the sea to change constantly, every wave is affected by what's around it, and what's around shapes each wave. In the words of the mathematician Blaise Pascal, can we conceive a circular relation? "One cannot know the parts if the whole is not known, but one cannot know the whole if the parts are not known."[15] Can we simultaneously comprehend the whole and the parts?

Instead of fixating again on this wave or that, can we focus on the relationship between the waves? We spoke about how the system is dynamic and is constantly changing. Can we focus on the process that results in this dynamic quality? Can we focus on the collision, collaboration, and conversation between these different parts? Every such conversation results in a new conception of the whole, and this affects future conversations. In a sense, the whole and the part dichotomy falls apart because there is a dynamic connectedness. What would you then term as the whole, and what is the part? The parts influence what the whole is and vice-versa. Fixed beliefs of what constitutes the whole and what constitutes the part no longer remain valid. We have to abandon our search for a wave.

If we let go of the fixedness of different objects, we see how we constantly construct different wholes based on the dynamics of different parts, which are again affected in the same way as the wholes are. For instance, take the notion of *I*. It is something we use easily, without much consideration. The word *I* refers to a fixed notion of the self that is independent of the situation one is in. It is independent of context. But what is the definition of *I*?

Is it your body? Your body has millions of bacteria that are constantly changing the constitution of your body. As you breathe in and out, the composition of these bacteria changes.[16] Would you think that you are changing every second? Or for that matter, are you the same in your workplace, in your home, in the arms of a loved one, and in a situation when you are faced with stress? In Japanese, the word *I* is not often used. Instead

Japanese has many words for *I*, depending on the audience and context. For instance, a man talking about himself in relation to his buddies would use *boku* or *ore*.[17] The context of a father is different from the context of a child talking to her family. The connection between the context and you changes who you are, just as you change the context you are in.[18]

If the ideas of whole and part become more fluid, what can we hold on to to understand what is going on? What do we call this process that causes different parts to interact constantly, changing and modifying themselves as well as the whole they constitute? The constant tension? A dynamic, continuous, and layered process? Can we conceive it as a dialogue?

On Dialogue

The root of the word *dialogue* lies in *dia* (which means "across") and *logos* (which is "knowledge"). A constant dialogue, a back and forth between the currents and countercurrents, gives rise to complex and dynamic behavior. A dialogue is not just a conversation between two entities, which implies an exchange. Rather, it shapes and is shaped by the entities participating in the dialogue.

A dialogue resonates with Pascal's idea that "One cannot know the parts if the whole is not known, but one cannot know the whole if the parts are not known." Rather, what we can attempt to understand is the dialogue that goes on. The result of this dialogue could be that the whole is more than, less than, or equal to the sum of its parts.[19] This is because instead of focusing on the parts or the whole, we are trying to focus on the relationship that mediates between them and transforms them.

When it comes to designing, a dialogue is characterized by a crucial quality. For instance, you design the idea of *I* based on different contexts. There

Figure 3.1
A dialogue.

is a negotiation between different threads that make who you are and helps you arrive at an idea of *I*. A dialogue implies that a difference is involved. A dialogue between identical entities is akin to a cellular automata—a grid where every cell assumes a color based on the colors of the cells adjacent to it. However, we are referring to a situation where the dialogue causes a change not just in color but in the very cells themselves. It is a dialogue that causes difference and that dwells in difference. And it is not just difference; it is difference married to plurality. It is not just many, and it is not just variety. It is a confluence of both. It is diversity. Our conception of designing requires and calls for diversity.

We conceive of a dialogue as a constant and dynamic process. The dialogue does not end; it does not have a full stop but pauses at different points of time. These pauses are what we term *temporary closures*. If we let go of the fixedness of objects, then what we have is a temporal understanding of the state of the dialogue the object is undergoing, and that state is captured in temporary closure. For instance, at every second, it is not possible for us to constantly dwell on the changing nature of *I*. Rather, at a certain point of time, the dialogue results in a temporary closure, which is what you perceive as the sense of yourself.

We tried to understand the characteristic and the behavior of the system a little while ago when we adopted a Cartesian approach. If we view a system as being characterized by a dialogue, what is its behavior like? The behavior is also a dialogue because there is no linear relationship between cause and effect where you can say, "This is the characteristic of the system, and this is the behavior." Rather, it is recursive. At every level, what we encounter is a dialogue. And so whether we discuss designing, the study of designing, or understanding a designer, we will adopt the same approach— that of a dialogue.

Dialogue and Designing

At the heart of a conception, where designing is conceived as dialogue, lies context. As artifact changes, context will change too and vice-versa. This dialogue involves the designers, too.

In chapter 2, we present different approaches that focus on the individual designer. There also are approaches that grapple with the social aspect

Figure 3.2
Designing involves a dialogue between the artifact and its context.

Figure 3.3
Designing involves a dialogue between the individual and the social.

Figure 3.4
Designing involves a dialogue between diverse disciplines.

of designing—how negotiations and discussions shape the designing process. The idea is not to flatten all individuals into an amorphous social entity or to see the individual as decontextualized. Instead of focusing on either the individual or the social, a conception of a dialogue allows us to focus on both simultaneously. How does the individual affect the social and vice-versa? Think of a tug of war. Every individual's strength is important, and yet at the same time, the individual's behavior is shaped by the group's behavior.

A dialogue, as described before, implies that designing necessarily requires multiple perspectives, multiple knowledge bases, multiple points of view. Any designing activity is necessarily transdisciplinary: it is a dialogue among different disciplines.

Not privileging one discipline over the other—rather, not privileging one kind of knowledge over the other—is the crux to realizing a complex view of designing. We are more used to respecting explicit knowledge—what we see in literature and other media. But there is implicit knowledge that cannot be captured in such a format, which also is important to design. For example, there is knowledge gained by experience, knowledge passed on from one generation to the next, and knowledge passed on through songs and children's tales. Every bit of such knowledge is required to design and to study designing because the knowledge is crucial to understanding context. Context has everything to do with being human, and being human is not just about what can be articulated in words and calibrated through machines.

Christopher Jones, who championed design methodology in the 1960s, later repudiated it and called for disavowing fragmentation:

> To solve the problems created by the specialization of the craft process, its fragmentation into a growing number of professions each highly specialized, requires more than a change in methods of thinking and of modeling. It requires an ability we do not yet have, the ability to communicate fully and quickly across the barriers that separate professions and which isolate their thinking from the experience of users. Perhaps it requires the disbanding of our tradition of separating planning from using, and a return to much less specialized, and more integrated, forms of responsibility and work. Certainly it needs some really fresh thinking about how to use computers and communication media. Our efforts so far to organize life at the scale of the system seem to rely not on rethinking the aims and purposes and modes of operation of activities like transport, education, medical treatment, housing, telecommunications, etc. All we have done so far is to homogenize to force life to fit increasingly standardized systems that are simple to design but insensitive to how it feels to use them. Our excuse, as professionals, as non-persons, is "I only work here." It's clear to me that no big change is possible till we change ourselves and our ideas.[20]

Designing as dialogue calls for disciplines to talk with each other and for less fragmentation, and it resonates with what physicist John Ziman describes as "post-academic science." Given that science has to tackle complex problems, he, too, calls for a pluralistic approach:

> The world of practice does not carve itself up neatly along the joints between the academic disciplines. In the context of application, all problems require a multi-disciplinary approach. Every important technological development—the transistor, antibiotics, nuclear weapons—combines ideas and techniques from all

over the academic map. If we have enough imagination, we can see this is equally true for research into fundamentals, such as the origins of life or the workings of the brain. The most radical feature of post-academic science could be its unself-conscious pluralism. It will welcome conceptual diversity and not be fearful of possible inconsistencies. If an untidy mixture of theory and practice, computer simulations and numerical data turns out to be the best available solution to a particular problem—so what?[21]

We see the dialogue in designing as a continuous process of refinement, and therefore there is no idea of a perfect design. Rather, what we have are temporary closures, which are pauses before the design continues. Thus, when conceived as a dialogue, designing is a constantly evolving and dynamic process involving the designers, context, and the artifact, which is punctuated by temporary closures.

Dialogue and the Designer

What a transdisciplinary approach involving designing as dialogue implies is that people who have expertise in different disciplines will come together to collaborate with each other. Such a collaboration is underlined by mutual respect. In his *Five Minds for the Future*, educationist Howard Gardner talks about different minds people should have to be successful in today's world,[22] one of them being the "respectful mind." He says: "It is recognizing that the world is composed of people who look different, think differently, have different belief and value systems, and that we can no longer be hermits and live in complete isolation." For us, the respectful mind denotes bringing such an attitude to designing, where each one is respectful of the other person's disciplinary background. It is not just sufficient to bring different people to the table. It is necessary for them to break bread with each other.

The question now is, "Who should be invited to the table?" And the answer is, "Anyone who is affected by the design and anyone who has insights into the context that affects them." Essentially, everyone is a designer. Everyone has some knowledge to offer to make the design contextual, meaningful, and richer.

Even with an individual designer who is designing by himself or herself in a garage, there is a dialogue. We design in collaboration with who we were and who we are now—our past selves and our present selves, our multiple identities, the knowledge we have and the knowledge we accumulate

INDIVIDUAL   INDIVIDUAL

Figure 3.5
Designers in dialogue with themselves.

afresh, the different disciplines we are learned in. All of these are in a constant dialogue with each other.

Moreover, given such a conception of a designer, there is no split between the creative and the analytical, the practitioner and the theorist, the doer and the thinker. To put it more succinctly, there is no divide between the mind and the body. Such a conception of a designer parallels Vitruvius's idea of someone who knows the practical arts as well as the theory behind it—someone who has an idea of the how, what, and why. Seen in this fashion, all of us are designers because we all draw from different knowledge bases that we have to design. Each of us has something to offer, a perspective drawn from experience and education, and each of us shares that dialogical relationship with the material world.

If everyone is a designer, then the study of designing is a liberal art, which according to its classical definition, is a subject that any free (liberated) citizen should study, understand, and explore. Instead of boxing disciplines into hermetically sealed compartments (such as sciences, arts, crafts, and law), designing demands synthesis. Open up the seals, and let the disciplines flow into each other. As we plumb the depths of our own fields of study, we will also broaden and learn from one another.

In some literature, a designer is referred to as a T-person, someone who understands a particular field in depth and can also synthesize across different streams. Thus, a designer has to have what Gardner[23] refers to as the disciplined mind, synthesizing mind, and creative mind. The disciplined mind comes with expertise in a particular discipline's tradition of thought. A synthesizing mind can understand and relate across disciplines. A creative mind can articulate fresh ways of seeing. It is the same view propounded by the Bauhaus and others—the conception of a designer as an advanced generalist rather than a narrow specialist. Designers are in constant dialogue with themselves and others. They are reflective practitioners.

Let us tell you about the story of a young mechanical engineer whom we met during an internship project and who did not believe in such a conception of a designer. He was asked to go out for fieldwork and collect data for a research project. After a few days of braving the hot summer streets of Bangalore, the intern came back to the office and said that he wanted to do some real work. On being asked to clarify what he meant, he said he wanted to work on computational modeling. The days of his internship were passing by in a blur of questionnaires, and he had not yet spent any time in front of a computer. He was getting nervous because when he applied for jobs later on, he had to demonstrate that he had created computational engineering models.

When asked about his fieldwork experience, he said he had been on a trip to interview people who made *agarbattis* (incense sticks) to understand about their livelihoods. When asked how they made these *agarbattis*, the young engineer explained the process. When asked if he could make a device that would help these people make *agarbattis* faster, the young engineer laughed at what he thought was a joke.

But he was faced with a challenge—to make a device that would help the women making *agarbattis* work faster without compromising on the quality. The young engineer continued to think it was a joke.

Some weeks passed, and what had started out as a lark had become an obsession. The would-be mechanical engineer worked with carpenters and friends to design an *agarbattis*-making machine. He had sent his fieldwork supervisors photos of this machine along with a letter that expressed an honest surprise and gratitude that this experience had made him look at engineering from a new perspective. He realized that trying to design such a machine without talking to the women entrepreneurs—to understand the economics of their business and the anthropology, sociology, and plain common sense that it required—would have been a theoretical exercise, devoid of any practical significance. The engineer had had his first lesson in what it means to design.

Dialogue and Society

What kind of a society would we design if we had a dialogue? Everyone who is affected by design would participate, not in a superficial manner but in full measure.[24] The goal of this dialogue would be to understand and explore how design affects us and how we are shaped by it. By bringing in this knowledge, we can change the way design is done. A dialogue internalizes and makes explicit the idea that we are shaped by and give shape to the world around us.

The core idea of a republic is that people have a say in what happens to them. It implies reclaiming in full measure this dialogue between humans and the human-made. We need a new constitution where we talk about how we have a say in what affects us, how we can explore the choices of what is designed, how we can participate in the design and be heard.

The Story of Designing So Far

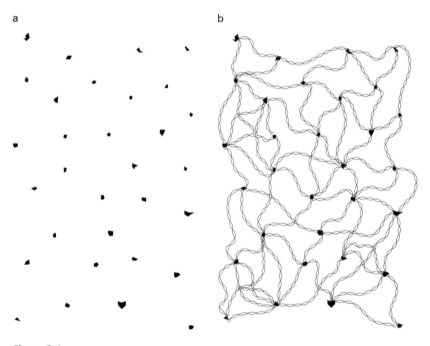

Figure 3.6
(a) Diverse people come together and (b) have a dialogue.

Designers:
DIALOGUE BETWEEN THE INDIVIDUAL AND SOCIAL

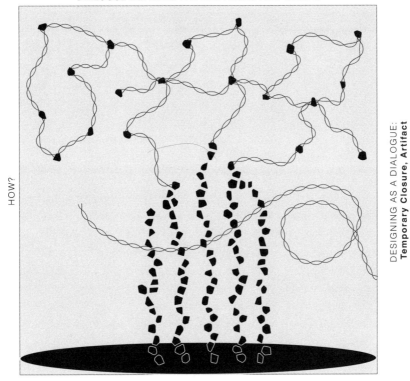

PEOPLE ARE AT THE HEART OF DESIGNING
CONTEXT IS CRITICAL

Figure 3.7
Designing as dialogue.

4   A New Vocabulary

Locke, in the seventeenth century, postulated (and rejected) an impossible language in which each individual thing, each stone, each bird and each branch, would have its own name; Funes once projected an analogous language, but discarded it because it seemed too general to him, too ambiguous. In fact, Funes remembered not only every leaf of every tree of every wood, but also every one of the times he had perceived or imagined it.

—Jorge Luis Borges, "Funes the Memorious"

In chapter 3, we characterize designing as a dialogue. Seeing designing as a dialogue lets us conceive of designing as a dynamic, continuously transformative act that in turn affects and changes those who participate in the dialogue. The dialogue is a recursive motif that appears at different levels through which we study designing.

In this chapter, we stare at, poke, prod, and analyze dialogue in designing. We observe snapshots in time, we draw from different wells of thought, and we construct what can be best termed a bricolage—carefully chosen pieces that when joined together offer us a tantalizing whole, a glimpse into a complex human activity.

The Dance of Design

In our conception of designing, the impulse to design is a human one. Therefore, to understand the dialogue in designing, we have to start with the people who design. What happens when people come together to create?

Imagine that you are sitting in your favorite chair in front of a dark stage. A spot of light seeks a figure you can sense in the darkness. A hip sways, and the essence of grace is distilled in that one movement. A body arcs from those sweat-stained arms to the nerves lining the neck, pulled by an unknown thread that is taut. The body seems drawn to another body that is gliding into that pool of light, too. Now what you see are two bodies that almost touch, enough for their breaths to commune with the same rhythm.

In that moment, time shatters. Space rearranges itself, and you cannot see one or the other in isolation any more. It is as though the landscape in front of you has altered permanently. You can no longer perceive the two bodies as separate individuals. They become one composite entity. The past seems like the uncertain stages of a rapid chemical reaction, and what you behold now has the grace of compounded stability. It is a unison that carves out space and time. It is now time to tango.

Every slight tap, every step, every breath is a negotiation with the music and the mood, with each other. Moments of order and disorder are punctuated by stillness. There is a persistent dialogue that flows like the rhythmic undercurrent. It governs but does not bind the complicated footwork. This dialogue, using a shared vocabulary of gestures, pressure, and movement, is constructed with purpose, a communing that determines the next move.

As time spins ahead with the tempo, the conversation races at the speed of thought, matched by moves that make you forget to breathe. You transcend the senses, and the experience now borders on the spiritual. What you witness is an effortless control over space and time that births meaning and infinite beauty. The unison is perfected, the conjoining complete.

Thus, the dialogue in designing can also be seen as a dance, with different people coming together to create paths into the unknown. In order to understand that dance, we journey to southern India, where a community of dancers has lived, breathed, and practiced dance for the past twenty-five years. This place is known as Nrityagram, a conjoining of *nritya* (dance) and *grama* (village). It is a *gurukul*, which is a place where students reside with their gurus or teachers and learn from them. With over two hundred students, Nrityagram has nurtured an artistic community dedicated to the study, practice, and teaching of Indian classical dance, especially Odissi.

The sinuous movements of Odissi, a classical Indian dance form, draw inspiration from temple sculptures in Orissa, a state in East India. Over the past twenty-five years, Nrityagram has developed a distinct style of Odissi that is practiced and perfected by the Nrityagram Dance Ensemble, which is internationally renowned and applauded by dance aficionados. To describe Nrityagram's art, life, and work is an exercise in futile hyperbole; no superlative seems sufficient. A *New York Times* reviewer echoes this sentiment when he says, "The only proper response to dancers this amazing is worship."[1]

In July 2012, we spoke to acclaimed choreographer and artistic director of Nrityagram, Surupa Sen, about creating *Samhara*, a collaboration between Nrityagram and Chitrasena Dance Company from Sri Lanka.[2] Heshma Wignaraja, the artistic director of the Chitrasena Dance Company, assisted Surupa Sen. The production was a dialogue between Odissi and Kandyan, a traditional dance form from Sri Lanka. After premiering at the Chowdiah Memorial Hall in Bangalore, India, in February 2012, *Samhara* toured the world. At the Joyce Theatre in New York, *Samhara* was performed to a packed audience that included the legendary dancer Mikhail Baryshnikov and renowned choreographer Mark Morris.

For us, the creation of *Samhara* was akin to designing, a dialogue between two different disciplines. The process of creating *Samhara* was, in our eyes, a metaphor for how the dialogue unfolds in designing.

Many Ways, Many Grounds of Seeing

The confluence of the two dance forms presents a challenge similar to two different disciplines coming together to design. Does it make sense to start with the similarities, or would the differences be a better starting point? According to Surupa Sen, there were both differences and similarities. Odissi comes from a classical tradition where poetry, music, and mythology are all attached to the dance, and therefore, it is multilayered. Kandyan is a ritual form where the music is rhythmic beating of drums, making it more athletic and dynamic but much less layered than Odissi. Therefore, to find a common substrate on which to build a conversation between the two forms was hard.

At the same time, there were similarities, she said. Kandyan was like a masculine counterpart of Odissi, and it seemed to have parallels to a tradition that arose out of the East Indian region, such as Chau, which is another athletic dance form. Although the basic wide stance, where dancers stand with their legs apart, bent at the knees, is similar in both the forms, Kandyan overall is more masculine. It could be because it used to be practiced only by males in places of worship. Therefore, to find that common ground was a challenge, she said.

It is the same challenge we face when different disciplines come together to design. What is the starting point? How do we build a common foundation?

If everyone saw the world in the same way, it would be quite simple. But is it so?

If you spoke to cognitive scientists in the late 1960s, they would have told you that it is indeed the case. There is one way of seeing the world. The reasoning behind such a view is as follows: People are endowed with brains, which process information. Humans are thus no different from machines because both can perform intelligent tasks as information processing systems. How does a brain or a machine process information? It is processed by representing information as symbols and by manipulating those symbols. By processing information thus, the brain solves different kinds of problems. Given a goal, the brain mobilizes its problem-solving capacity and searches through different alternatives by which it can reach that goal. Designing is thus nothing but an individual solving a problem.

If the same idea is applied to a group of people from different disciplines designing together (say, in an organization), the behavior of the organization is an aggregation of different individuals organized hierarchically. Early cognitive design research adopted this model and performed numerous studies of individual problem solving starting with design problems in architecture and fields in engineering. This worldview of designing led to the creation of expert systems in a number of fields in engineering.

But when we observe people designing, we realize that it is not as straightforward as the "mind as machine" metaphor that encapsulates the 1960s and 1970s vision of cognition.[3] For starters, designing is an exploration into the unknown.

Let us return to the creation of *Samhara*. When Surupa described the process of bringing together Kandyan and Odissi, her descriptions stressed the uncertainty of the process. She said that the dancers did not understand the process of her choreography, so she gave them tasks to do, which involved thinking about the dance. She saw the results and then told them what to do. "A lot of the time, they have absolutely no clue. They are floundering with me," she said. Even if she explained what her thought process was, the dancers were unsure what the outcome would be. "Because I am finding my way through it just as much as they are," she said. "But somehow I trust I will find my way."

In designing, too, there is a strong element of that uncertainty regarding the outcome. Yet there is a process underlying that journey, and although the outcome is unknown, expertise and experience are guides. The insights reveal themselves in doing, in creating, in the actual practice of designing. Just like Surupa's dance, designing relies on doing and is rooted in practice. In other words, it is situated, and one strand of cognition is called *situated cognition*, which explains such a conception of designing.[4]

Let us illustrate with an example. For instance, your father is putting together a new dish that involves him invoking his experience to identify the edible items in the fridge that can palatably go together, whereas a molecular gastronomist would use her knowledge of physics and chemistry to create a new dish. What is common to both designs is an ability to perceive patterns and articulate theories to explain what is common. These theories are particular and situational. Therefore, the way people perceive and understand is contextual. What this means for designing is that context is crucial, and we cannot flatten different perspectives stemming from different contexts into one uniform one-size-fits-all conception of an individual.

If cognition is situated and if the way we perceive the world depends on the situation we are embedded in, then where do we begin when we start designing together? Once again, what is the starting point?

Building a Common Ground

In Surupa's case, she discovered a starting point, a common ground, during the first workshop she did with both the Odissi and Kandyan dancers. Both cultures worshipped the elements, and she found a common language to express the elements through dance movements. Finding this common language was the starting point, and it helped the two distinct dance forms come together.

The process of building on the common ground involved the dancers listening to Surupa's ideas, working on reflecting those ideas through dance, and performing it back to her. The common ground grew in reworking those movements. The dancers' bodies, therefore, became a site for building a common ground.

In designing the material setting, the external representations of thought—such as gestures, symbolic representations, visual aids, and natural environment—play a crucial role in building a common ground. Cognition in designing thus can be seen as distributed between people and their material setting:

> The distributed cognition perspective aspires to rebuild cognitive science from the outside in, beginning with the social and material setting of cognitive activity, so that culture, context, and history can be linked with the core concepts of cognition.[5]

Distributed cognition is based on the premise that internal representations in the mind, whatever their status may be, interact with external representations. It is this interaction that leads to coordinating different activities among people and to tackle the problem at hand. External representations are a way to cope with the limitations of the ability to manipulate internal representations. For example, solving a large set of equations is not possible within your head, but writing down the calculations helps you tackle them easily. When you reread what you have written, you collaborate with your own self, and in this sense, cognition is distributed across time. Thus, the conception of designers collaborating with themselves over time (as mentioned in chapter 3) and having a dialogue with their self is underpinned by theories of distributed cognition.[6]

Building a Common Vocabulary

The process of building a common ground between different perspectives in designing takes time and effort. The dancers from Chitrasena Dance Company stayed in Nrityagram for the entire time that *Samhara* was choreographed. This close interaction meant that the process of creation could take its time, and both Surupa and Heshma Wignaraja, the artistic director of Chitrasena Dance Company who assisted Surupa in the choreography, could understand each other.

Heshma said that she and Surupa would have dinner together and talk over the section they were working on and Surupa's thoughts about the work they had done. She said that during these conversations she began to understand what Surupa sought from her, but Surupa would insist, "Don't give me what I like. Give me what works for you!"

According to Heshma, one of the major differences between Odissi and Kandyan lies in what accompanies the dance. Kandyan is married to the drum, and music and lyricism are in a way absent from the dance form. Although folk songs are used as part of the traditional dance, neither the musicality nor the meaning of the words in the songs' verses are used much in the dance. Traditional Kandyan can be likened to ballet, which is abstract movement in space. The drums give it a joyous and fiery energy. On the other hand, Odissi is accompanied by a vocalist, string instruments, wind instruments, as well as rhythm, making it more layered. Therefore, building a common ground meant finding a musical bridge.

According to Surupa, the challenge was in creating a soundscape that could blend the rhythm of Kandyan with Odissi. She gave the dancers exercises invoking the elements, and they performed the results back to her. For instance, the dancers would have to depict air or water, and she pushed them to discover a new vocabulary to depict these elements, which could evolve into a common language. "So you take the five elements, and you create the first substance. That was the idea," she said.

When the dancers go back to think about their exercises and discover a new language, there is a dialogue between the body and the mind, where the dancers' bodies perform two functions—mediation and a forging of a cognitive common ground between the people involved in the production. In designing, such mediators are referred to as boundary objects.

Boundary Objects

Boundary objects, a concept explained by social scientists Susan Leigh Star and James R. Griesemer, help coordinate between people from different disciplinary backgrounds. They exist at the boundaries of different disciplines. They do not require people to rewrite those disciplinary boundaries.

Consider a stuffed bird at the Museum of Vertebrate Zoology at the University of California, Berkeley.[7] Star and Griesemer studied different people in this museum as part of their work on boundary objects.

Annie Alexander, a passionate patron and administrator of the museum, who was also an amateur animal collector, had a problem: how could she engage people who had little or no interest in conservation (such as trappers and traders) in obtaining more species for the museum? Describing problems with a trapper who wanted to sell skins to the museum, the administrator said, "It seems next to impossible to persuade a trapper to kill an animal without whacking it on the head."[8]

Alexander was the museum's primary patron, and she funded salaries, provided for upkeep, and also acted as an administrator who managed operations. She was not a theoretical scientist, and her commitment to the museum stemmed from her commitment to conservation and educational philanthropy. As Susan Leigh Star and James R. Griesemer wrote in their paper "Institutional Ecology, 'Translations' and Boundary Objects: Amateurs and Professionals in Berkeley's Museum of Vertebrate Zoology, 1907–1939": "The museum was a way of preserving a vanishing nature, of making a record of that which was disappearing under the advance of civilization. For her, as for many social elites of the period, natural history was both a passionate hobby and a civic duty."[9] Such conservation efforts require the participation of amateur collectors, who contacted farmers, trappers, and others who could provide them with specimen. Star and Griesemer's essay talks about different people, including animals, professionals, and amateurs, who participate in scientific work.

On the one hand lies the grisly act of killing an animal, and on the other lies a commitment to conservation and educational philanthropy—and different perspectives have different takes on the ethics and the imperatives of the situation. By citing this example, we are not taking a stance here. We intend it to be an exemplar to further talk about boundary objects and to continue the dialogue on how seeing the museum only as a clinical space for research and conservation is to ignore other actors involved in the process.

For example, a zoologist and a trapper would see a bird sitting on a tree very differently. For the zoologist, the bird is of a particular species and will probably fit nicely into an empty space in the museum. For the trapper, it is a nonedible creature that won't fetch any money. How can the two coordinate?

Star and Griesemer, who studied the museum, tell us about the concept of a boundary object.[10] Suppose that you ask the trapper and the zoologist to share a boundary object (say, a model stuffed animal) and both agree on it. This means that the trapper will be careful with the animal and the zoologist will feel comfortable that the species is maintained intact. The boundary object thus manages the tension between these different viewpoints, helps in negotiation, and serves to support cooperation between participants. For example, if the trapper is not interested in either conservation or environment, money for the specimen is decided as a basis of participation without agreement about the classification of the object and actions:

Discipline 1	Boundary object	Discipline 2

Earlier we spoke about the second function performed by the dancers' bodies: they helped create a shared understanding. In other words, they performed a cognitive function too. Similarly, boundary objects have to rest on what we term a *cognitive scaffold* to transcend disciplinary boundaries to instill a shared understanding.

To understand more about boundary objects and the cognitive scaffold they rest on, let us crash into the retirement party of a mechanical engineer at a power equipment firm.[11] The mechanical engineer has stepped down after a long and fruitful career. The person who was supposed to take over his position received another offer and failed to join the firm. As a result, by the time the vacancy was filled, the mechanical engineer had gone on a long-awaited vacation to Papua New Guinea. The new recruit decided the job would not be difficult. All the mechanical engineer did was to evaluate the electrical engineers' design specifications and finalize a design specification document for drafting and manufacturing.

Electrical engineer's design specifications	Sent to	Mechanical engineer (who evaluates and finalizes the document)	Sent to	Drafting and manufacturing

Within a month, there was chaos in the firm. No one understood how the retired mechanical engineer, currently training his binoculars on a bird of paradise in a rainforest, had done the job.

After receiving frantic messages from his colleagues on his answering machine, he returned to his office and his former desk and took out a diary. In this personal notebook was a classification of all the designs done over the past thirty years and personal copies of entire design folders for some designs that were unique in certain ways. The mechanical engineer had become a librarian. In other words, he was a curator of shared memory and a custodian of the House of Nine Muses.

He had evaluated the electrical engineers' design specifications with respect to the classifications in his book. This enabled him to verify the design and finalize a design specification document for drafting and manufacturing.

What is the role of this crucial classification system that the engineer had painstakingly handwritten in his notebook? It is a cognitive scaffold. The classification remained invisible to both the electrical engineers and the drafting and manufacturing folks. The retired mechanical engineer, who sat at the crossroads of information flow between the two groups, had provided a cognitive scaffold for these boundary objects (design and manufacturing specifications), a necessary link between the two groups.

Electrical engineer's design specifications	Sent to	Mechanical engineer (who evaluates and finalizes the document) using his personal classification system	Sent to	Drafting and manufacturing (which receives revised design specifications)
Design specifications: Boundary object		Personal classification system: Cognitive scaffold		Revised design specifications: Boundary object

A change in the boundary object requires a corresponding change in the cognitive scaffold supporting it. With the goal of increasing productivity in the workplace, computer-aided design (CAD) was introduced. One study found that CAD increased productivity by no more than 5 percent in the first year and that the real productivity growth took place after five years.[12] An interpretation of this study was that the use of CAD tools requires significant conceptual shifts because of the fundamental extension to manual procedures. These shifts are required because of the CAD tools' capacity to manipulate and compose structures of geometry, things not possible in manual drawing. This change requires a shift in the models of drafting and manufacturing engineers.

Another study found that the introduction of CAD introduced new classes of errors because of new sets of operations whose semantics were new to the user and not well understood. The primary observation here is that a technological shift in the creation of drawings (boundary objects) has created a conceptual shift with its attendant language and its interpretations (cognitive scaffolding), hence changing understanding of these boundary objects.[13]

Sometimes a boundary object acts like a cognitive scaffold when it becomes a link among one or more perspectives. The more the links the boundary object has to multiple perspectives, the more complex is the cognitive scaffold. The more complex the scaffold, the more tentative and fragile its status.

This brings us to the curious case of process N and process M, two transformer design processes that were used within the same company.[14] A transformer design process is the process through which the transformer moves from the design stage to the test stage. Design and manufacturing specifications are created at the design stage. Engineers evaluate these specifications using certain analytical tools and models. The design and manufacturing specifications are then sent to the test stage:

Design stage	Test stage
Boundary objects: Design and manufacturing specifications	
Cognitive scaffold: Analytical tools and manuals	

Now we come to the curious part. When transformers that had been designed through process N came to the test floor, their success rate was 60 percent. On the other hand, the success rate for process M was 98 percent. What accounted for this startling difference in performance?

The study revealed that the key to this difference was held in the hands of an engineer employed by the department in charge of process M. This engineer visited the manufacturing facility and the test facility every day to collect test data and performance data. This data was then fed to the analytical tools and manuals used to evaluate the specifications. This meant that any specification that came through process M was evaluated and could be used to predict the performance based on the most recent company-wide information on what caused failures. In the department in charge of process N, however, these updates were received almost two years later.

This meant those working on process N knew only what failures they were exposed to.[15] They often made ad hoc rules based on the little information they had. This led to costly rework, sometimes even after the devices were shipped.

The above example illustrates the fragility of boundary objects when they are not maintained to keep the different interpretations aligned through organizational and cultural dialogues.[16] The life of a boundary object occupies many niches in the dialogues between and among disciplines and perspectives. The boundary object and cognitive scaffolds are interrelated in the sense that scaffolds allow the boundary object to be interpreted. These cognitive scaffolds can be classifications in a discipline or in a specific context that serves a community of practice.[17] These boundary objects and cognitive scaffolds in many forms and media, in effect, are models (both encoded and physical) that serve the cognitive process that occurs at individual, distributed, social, and cultural levels.

We will henceforth refer to all boundary objects and cognitive scaffolds that serve cognition as models. Whether sketches, drawings, visuals, tables, charts, videos, audios, mathematical, or physical representations, they are all models. We create models, we design them, we have a dialogue with them in designing. Extending Donald Schön's idea of a reflective practitioner in a dialogue with herself, our idea of designing is that the individual and the social are in a dialogue with the models. All these entities involved in the dialogue evolve simultaneously. The dialogue is not linear but instead is emergent. It depends on the participants and their context.[18]

Creating a New Language

As the dialogue in designing unfolds and different disciplines begin to coordinate with each other through boundary objects, a shared common ground slowly emerges, articulated by a new shared language. In coming up with the new language, the disciplines themselves undergo a transformation as the dialogue informs the disciplines too. When describing the process of how the dialogue between Odissi and Kandyan unfolded, Surupa's choreographic process resonates with the process of designing. The process brought together rhythm (which is the lifeblood of Kandyan) and music for both Odissi and Kandyan to have a dialogue that transformed Kandyan by "leaps and bounds," according to Heshma. "That was the biggest new ground that we broke on our part to really see how Kandyan works with music," she said.

Speaking about the transformation, she elaborated: "But then when you see the show [*Samhara*] after all that, the Kandyan sections are very different from the way we would have performed them here [in Sri Lanka]." She adds, "New ways of moving, new rhythm patterns—look like another form but are not. Everywhere there are definite connections to it being purely Kandyan. That was the most exciting part for me to understand how far can you throw yourself."

The process of creating choreography and finding common ground between Odissi and Kandyan gives us a sense that in the back and forth there is a sense of building a new language together. As Heshma says, the Kandyan performed in *Samhara* almost looks like another form, but it is not.[19] Here, language is not just a medium of communication. Rather, it is more like what the psycholinguist Herbert H. Clark calls a joint activity. In a joint activity, two or more people perform actions together. Thus, two people tangoing together are seen as a pair rather than as two individuals dancing. Functioning as a composite unit is a characteristic of a joint action.

When one person dances alone, he or she performs autonomous actions. When two dance together—even though they continue to dance on their own—their actions become participatory. Joint actions comprise participatory actions, and the reverse is also true. As Clark says, "we can look at a joint action either way—as a whole made up of parts, or as parts making up the whole" (as with our conception of a dialogue, the whole and part are not distinct but are constantly formed and reformed by the act of dialogue).[20]

Describing how Kandyan was transformed and yet remained the same through the dialogue, Heshma said that although the dance was created with the language she knew best, which was Kandyan, the process of working with Surupa made that language "completely fresh." During the process of designing, different models (including sketches, drawings, visuals, tables, charts, videos, audios, mathematical, gestural, and symbolic) become the vocabulary of the language that develops in designing. Both the models and the language help in mediating as well as developing a cognitive common ground.[21]

The Dance Revisited

When we describe designing as dialogue in chapter 3, we speak about the dialogue between the artifact and the context, the dialogue between the individual and the social and parts and wholes, and the dialogue between different disciplines. Our conception of designing is based on discovering the ecology of design in terms of designing as a dialogical process that is directed at achieving a desired outcome. The theories of distributed and situated cognition underpin our understanding of designing as a contextual process—a dialogue. Cognition and design are inseparable at all levels of designing. We do not exist only as individuals but live in a network that encompasses the social aspect of our lives, and designing is a cognitive act—a dialogue between the individual and the social. It is a dialogue that takes place in an interacting network of actors, disciplines, perspectives, models, and languages to achieve a goal in a given social context. We introduce the idea of mediators of this dialogical process, which enables a cognitive common ground that includes models such as sketches, drawings, visuals, tables, charts, videos, audios, mathematical, and physical representations. We describe the theory of boundary objects (drawn from the sociology of work) and ethnographic studies that led us to understand cognitive scaffolds to describe the functions that models perform. Over time, as the dialogue in designing unfolds, these models become the vocabulary of a common language that underlies the joint activity (drawn from cognitive linguistics) that is designing.[22]

Seen in another way, in this chapter, we design a model—a theoretical base that underpins our conception of a dialogue—and in doing so develop a nascent language to describe the dialogue in designing. (As you can see, we are fond of recursion.)

Given the central importance of models to our understanding of designing, in the next chapter, we turn the spotlight on these models. What are models? How are they created, managed, and reconstituted? How do they persevere? What are the implications for practice? These are some of the questions the next chapter addresses.

During the interview, Surupa said: "Not all the information is relevant. A lot of the time what choreography and creation are is how much and how well you edit." Keeping in mind this piece of advice, we have not included a lot of other associated theories in the main body of the chapter, and we have included extensive footnotes for readers interested in exploring further.

The Story of Designing So Far

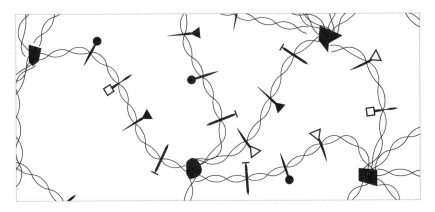

Figure 4.1
The dialogue in designing is mediated by models, which include boundary objects and cognitive scaffolds.

Designers:
DIALOGUE BETWEEN THE INDIVIDUAL AND SOCIAL

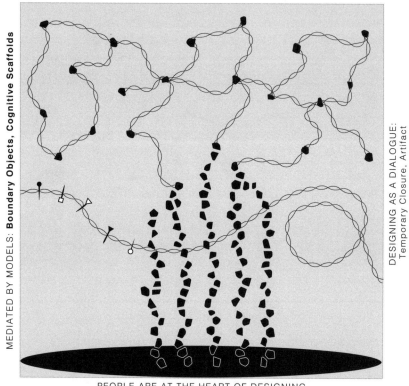

PEOPLE ARE AT THE HEART OF DESIGNING
CONTEXT IS CRITICAL

Figure 4.2
How the dialogue in designing unfolds.

5 Design Detritus

Our entire linear and accumulative culture collapses if we cannot stockpile the past in plain view.

—Jean Baudrillard, *Simulacra and Simulation*

What is common to the Australian coastline, the beaches of Bali, and those of Rio de Janeiro? The answer: plastic waste. What is common to the Agbogbloshie commercial district on the river in Accra, Ghana, and Seelampur in Delhi, India? The answer: electronic waste. Our understanding of designing cannot be complete without inquiring into what happens in the afterlife of artifacts and how we as designers are responsible. In this chapter, we dwell on waste, and in doing so we continue to unpack the process of designing as a dialogue between humans, the material world, and the natural world.

Design Detritus

Have you tried Indian-style pickled mango or limes or even prawns? They may be quite different from the North American pickled gherkins, but the basic principle remains the same: a vegetable or a fruit is marinated in salt to extend its life. The Indian spice box is very rich and diverse and includes a large collection of spices, especially powdered red chilies that are added in the making of certain pickles. Probably one of the most evocative odes to the Indian pickle is in Salman Rushdie's novel, *Midnight's Children* (1981), where he describes the Braganza pickle factory and its owner Mary Pereira, apparently inspired by a real-life factory called Ferns Pickles in Mumbai.

Although most households, even in urban India, used to prepare and consume homemade pickles, increasingly fewer do so. For one, pickling is not an easy process. Making mango pickle, for instance, requires carefully choosing raw mangoes, washing and drying them, peeling and slicing them, and cutting them into same-sized cubes. These cubes are then sun-dried and pickled with a variety of spices. Errant fingers of children and adults in the household are forbidden from touching the work in progress because even a tiny bit of moisture can spoil the entire batch of pickles.

Once made, the pickles used to be stored in porcelain jars. A small quantity was spooned out for daily use, and the main jar was stored on a high shelf, far from the reach of tiny fingers. The pickle jar enjoyed a special relationship with the household. You knew its antecedents, you knew the effort that went into its making, and you knew its value. It was almost always women who made these pickles, and the burden of housework and the attendant gender politics went a long way in making these pickles possible. Today, most households continue to consume them, but the porcelain jars have been replaced by factory-bottled pickles in plastic jars. Although buying pickles is much less work than making them, the human relationship we used to share with these objects has been lost.

The readymade pickles in plastic jars are easy to get and consume, and the jars are easy to then throw away. The design philosophy followed is to use and throw away. These plastic bottles are designed to crack and break, and the brittle plastic that they are made from is not reusable. In a way, the bottles are designed to be rubbish.

This abridged story of pickles and their bottles is not a call to return to the times when women cooked and made pickles all day long. Far from it. It is a plea to look at the interconnectedness of different issues. How do we reimagine something as simple as pickle making in a way that we do not add to design detritus and yet at the same time do not lose the advantages that readymade pickles offer us?

It is not an easy question to answer. Yet there are many questions like these that we designers need to contend with. How do we approach issues that Rittel and Weber referred to as wicked problems? These problems are too complex for one discipline to have all the answers. For starters, the pickle problem would need a dialogue between the economics of the pickle industry, critical theory,[1] sociology of work, environmental science, and chemistry. We need a dialogue between different disciplines and a way to mediate those dialogues.

Not only do we need to bring different disciplines together, but we also need to bridge the gap between theory and practice because designing is about doing and not just about understanding. If we consider theories as abstractions and practice as doing, then both theory and practice contribute to knowledge building. Both of them are sources of information and, in turn, knowledge. How can we engender a meaningful dialogue between knowledge that resides in theory and the insights gained from practice by drawing from different disciplines? In this chapter, we focus deeply on dialogues that build bridges across theories from different disciplines and practice, how these dialogues unfold, and what is needed to support them and to keep track of their health. To delve into these questions, we take you through a project on rubbish undertaken by Fields of View,[2] a not-for-profit research organization in Bangalore.

Let's Talk Rubbish!

In April 2017, a landslide in the outskirts of Colombo, Sri Lanka, killed at least thirty-two people and destroyed nearly 150 homes.[3] This was not an ordinary mountain of earth and vegetation but a massive mountain of rubbish, a result of continued dumping of refuse from the city, that had come crashing down. Imagine it for a second—a mountain of festering garbage. In mid-March of 2017, a similar tragedy occurred in Addis Ababa in Ethiopia, killing around sixty-five people.[4]

Cities in India face a similar problem of waste. Landfills are omnipresent in cities like Bangalore (Mandur, Mavallipura, Lakshmipura, Bingipura), Mumbai (Deonar, Mulund, Kanjurmarg), Delhi (Ghazipur, Okhla, Bhalswa), Chennai (Perungudi, Kodungaiyur, Tiruvottiyur), Trivandrum (Vilappisala), and Ahmedabad (Pirana).[5]

What can the team at Fields of View do to address the problem of urban waste in India? This question was the starting point for the team, and its members started going through academic papers, newspaper articles, and other literature. It became apparent very early on that this complex problem could not be boxed into just one silo. The team needed insights from different disciplines to understand the problem.

How Do We Make Sense?

Let us look at the landscape of urban waste in a city. The different kinds of waste include solid waste, e-waste, biowaste, organic waste, and construction waste. Each of these waste categories comes with its own set of complexities and challenges. The flow of solid waste is different from the flow of construction waste. E-waste is an entirely different subject altogether.

Now think of the different kinds of disciplines that provide insights into the problem of urban waste. Environmental science, economics, engineering, sociology, and law and policy are just some of the fields that provide insights into urban waste. Therefore, relying on any one discipline alone would not be sufficient. The Fields of View team needed bits and pieces from different disciplinary fields and had to stitch them together.

The team had to consider not just formal sources of knowledge (available in the form of academic papers, newspaper reports, and books) but other sources (such as discussion groups in social media sites, blogs, and interviews with people who were not necessarily experts). It needed a way to take all these different nuggets of information gleaned from different fields and sources and stitch them together in a comprehensible manner through a dialogue.

In chapter 4, we speak of models that mediate the process of design. What the Fields of View team ended up doing, in stitching together different scraps of wisdom into a cogent and coherent whole, was to build different models.

Models help in two critical ways: they help us combine bits and pieces of knowledge from different disciplines and sources, and they help us bridge the gap between the theoretical world of abstractions and practice. We design these models not just to understand the system but to chart a way forward and hone our understanding. Models are thus a site of understanding and negotiating the next step of the design process.

We now arrive at our working definition of models. Models are epistemological devices, the site of the dialogue in designing. The dialogue can be between or across different disciplines, between different people, and between theory and practice, where models encode the current consensual understanding.[6]

What do we mean by epistemological devices?

As Shakespeare puts it in *As You Like It*, what if we could be like someone who "finds tongues in trees, books in the running brooks, sermons in
stones, and good in everything"? What if we were able to look around us
to find streams of knowledge from different sources and draw from these
streams to design? We would need to carve a path for this water to flow
unhindered. Relying on a theoretical formulation would mean having to
practice a certain economy of information, which is not feasible when it
comes to design because design requires drawing from different theories.
Thus, models allow us to manage different levels and amounts of information. They are devices that allow us to construct and reconstruct knowledge, ask questions, and seek specific answers.[7]

The act of modeling has an experimental core. These models are in a
state of constant becoming, as though they are made of clay. They are mal-
leable and flexible, and for this reason, they become the substrate for the
act of dialogue between different disciplines or between the designer and
the world.

In Fields of View's project on waste, the team had to understand different kinds of waste in the city to see what the focus of the project could be.
In order to do that, the team created different kinds of models. For instance,
a paper on e-waste was mashed up with geographical locations of areas that
deal with e-waste in the city, and links were overlaid to the e-waste policy and the gaps in implementation. A model helped the team create this
picture, this story, a space for sense making, which helped team members
decide whether the focus was on e-waste or not. To reiterate, models help
in both understanding (by drawing from different disciplines in a cogent
manner) and negotiating the next step in the design process (thus bridging
theory and practice).[8]

A Decentralized System

At about this time, the Fields of View team met Nalini Shekar, cofounder of
Hasiru Dala, an organization of waste workers that works toward improving the livelihood opportunities and quality of life of waste workers. Nalini
took the team deeper into the solid waste system in Bangalore.

Bangalore used to follow a centralized system of waste management
where the urban local body coordinated waste collection and disposal.
The city's waste was dumped in its outskirts, near villages such as Mandur

and Mavallipura. Eventually, the citizens in those villages began protesting against this practice. The situations in these villages had become dire: the groundwater was dark due to the leachate from the dumped waste, and the smell around the area was foul. On days when hospital waste was dumped, the stench was so acute that people could not even eat. Civil society groups supported the citizens from these villages in their protests. In 2012, the High Court ordered the urban local body to move to a decentralized system of waste management.[9]

In the new decentralized system, everyone would segregate the waste they produce. When waste was segregated into different categories at the source, wet waste or organic waste was to be made into compost at the household or neighborhood level. Any wet waste collected would be sent to the compost development corporation in the outskirts of Bangalore.

Dry, recyclable waste was to be sent to dry waste collection centers (DWCCs), which were to be set up by the urban local body in every ward (the smallest administrative unit in an Indian city). They were the physical embodiment of the new decentralized systems. These dry waste collection centers would collect all dry waste and sell it to recyclers. The land for setting up these centers would be provided by the government, and support in terms of electricity and water would also be provided.

People who were formerly in the informal sector were managing many DWCCs in Bangalore at the time of this project.[10] They had become managers of DWCCs with the assistance of civil society groups such as Hasiru Dala. Such DWCC managers had intimate knowledge of waste, including how different kinds of waste could be sorted and segregated and how maximum value from waste could be realized. In a way, the success of this new decentralized system of solid waste management relied on the success of these DWCCs. The team now had a new focus in the project—solid waste management in Bangalore, with a focus on the decentralized system and DWCCs.

The project team's focus was now solid waste, so it created an in-depth model of solid waste flows and actors in Bangalore combining both desk and field research. The team undertook field visits to understand the landscape of solid waste management better. From making a visit to the Karnataka Compost Development Center to trailing garbage trucks across the city, team members refined their understanding of what the situation was. They spoke to more experts. With every piece of additional information, their model became more refined, a tapestry of different streams of knowledge.

Dialogue: Nature, the Material World, and Us

Working on waste made the team grapple with how nature, the material world, and humans are interconnected, but the extent of the problem of waste showed how broken this relationship was. Researching the problem helped team members realize that this was an ongoing and omnipresent dilemma, repeated everywhere like a chorus: should they focus on the social aspect of waste, its economic aspect, or its environmental aspect?

Some analyses focused only on the economics of waste management. Some saw it as an environmental issue. A few studies focused on the social and cultural aspects of the problem. Consider the DWCCs themselves. If citizens segregate their waste and send their dry waste to DWCCs, more waste gets recycled, and thereby less waste is dumped in landfills. If waste in landfills is reduced, there is less leachate, less groundwater pollution, and fewer health risks. Thus, DWCCs have an environmental role to play.

DWCCs also have a social aspect. For starters, in India, the issue of waste is intimately linked to the caste system entrenched in the Indian society, and waste picking is traditionally bound to the lowest caste, which exacerbates the stigma against people in the informal waste sector.[11] Even though informal sector workers are responsible for managing up to 30 percent of solid waste collection and subsequently recycling it, their work was acquiring visibility only now. DWCCs help make the efforts of the informal sector workers visible because several DWCCs are managed by and are staffed with former informal sector workers. When informal workers are employed in a DWCC, they receive training and work papers from the urban local body, thereby giving them formal recognition.

Moreover, DWCCs provide context for citizens to become more active and conscious about waste management because it provides space for citizens to send their segregated dry waste. Last but not the least, DWCCs are a marketplace for dry waste. Dry waste is bought and sold to recyclers, there are operation costs and other associated costs, and the goal is to make a profit at the end of the day.

As designers, the team needed to look at all the three aspects of DWCCs—social, environmental, and economical. Rather than focusing on only one, the team had to focus on the dialogue between the material world, the natural world, and us.

That is where models help. We can bring together these different spheres of knowledge and insights and look at how they affect each other. For instance, the team created a model of the flow of dry waste and the actors involved across different times. They mapped the relationship between the actors in terms of economics and power structures. Then they created a detailed model of how DWCCs operated, including all their activities and functions.

The team could use a particular model to communicate with others about the project. It could use a different model internally to discuss and debate. Different models operated at different levels of abstractions, and they could speak to different audiences.

Seen in another way, the models allowed the team to manipulate information and ask questions at different levels of abstraction. There is an element of zooming in and out between detailed information and reduced information, and models help designers traverse through these different levels.[12]

A Playground of Models

The next problem was also unique: how could the team manage these different models at different levels of abstraction? For instance, some models focused on actors, others focused on macro-level information at the city level. Some models mixed both these levels.

Designing, however, requires that we constantly shape and reshape models as though they were made of clay. What we then need is a space where we can build and rebuild models or what we term *conceptual flat space*.[13]

Given the scale of the project, a drawing board was the conceptual flat space where the team could compose different models that were drawn from different sources of knowledge. For instance, they could elaborate on the economic and power relations between different actors involved in solid waste to compose a fresh model. The team then broke down this model of different actors to focus only on institutional actors, a new model. It overlaid this model with the existing legislation on waste. In essence, team members created a playground where they could shape and reshape these models.

The easiest way to understand what a conceptual flat space implies is with the help of a domestic example. Take a look at your kitchen shelf, where salt, sugar, oils, spices, pulses, lentils, and grains are all stacked in rows. Suppose you transfer all these to the floor but in no particular arrangement or order. If someone walks into your kitchen when it is looking like this, they probably will think they that you are in the middle of a spring cleaning session. But to get to our point, what is on the floor is a conceptual flat space. In order to cook, you pick and choose what you want and arrange these items in a particular order (first the oil, then the spices, and then the salt), and in doing so you create the order needed to cook a specific dish. When you are done, you return all the ingredients to the floor, including the dish you cooked, or in other words collapse back into the flat space. Now, by picking different dishes and additional ingredients, you could form different meals for different tastes and nutrition needs.

We create and use different permutations and combinations of ingredients and recipes while cooking. Different people might follow different steps to cook the same dish. The conceptual flat space allows for all of them to experiment, share their own arrangements, and look into what others have done too.

Conceptual flat space	
Ingredients	Arrangements (Different recipes)

This idea can be extended to any collection of parts—whether a filing system, your clothes cupboard, or a cross-country design collaboration.

Imagine if the project at hand involved five organizations, spread across all continents, and their focus was to look at e-waste flows across countries. These organizations would need to enable a conceptual flat space where all kinds of models (such as documents, videos, papers, blogposts, and sketches) could be stored and composed in myriad ways. The compositions become part of the conceptual flat space and so on. The conceptual flat space is how shared memory can be made actionable in the design process.

In chapter 2, we introduce the idea of the shared memory. It is our starting point to venture into how designing has been studied over the ages. Shared memory allows for such analysis because it is a storehouse of knowledge. And shared memory becomes the crucial link between theory and practice—because both theory and practice contribute to the shared memory. In essence, it becomes a site of dialogue between theory and practice. Models in designing contribute to and draw from the shared memory, and the conceptual flat space is a way for us to operationalize shared memory in new contexts.

Take Fields of View's project on waste, which drew on knowledge from urban planning, designing, economics, and a whole host of other fields. They created knowledge that cut across different disciplines, which they were adding back to the shared memory of designing because it is the repository of that horizontal knowledge that traverses across disciplinary boundaries.

What Do We Make?

As the Fields of View team began creating different models of the dry waste system in Bangalore and understood better how the system of DWCCs functioned and how its success was crucial to the success of the decentralized system, one question kept bothering the team: "Why weren't these DWCCs making a profit?" It was the same question Nalini from Hasiru Dala had left the team with. So what could be done to help the DWCCs make a profit? The team's focus was limited to those DWCCs that were managed by people who were formerly in the informal sector.

In their research, the Fields of View team identified two key reasons for DWCCs not making a profit: not many citizens segregated waste at the source, and not many knew about the existence of the DWCCs. Although models helped team members hone their understanding of the system, they were designers, and their intent was not just to understand but to create. Therefore, although they used different models to enhance their understanding of the problems both at theoretical and practical levels, they also needed to keep track of their objective of knowing what they were designing toward. They had models of the solid waste management system in Bangalore focusing on the economics of waste, a model of how DWCCs functioned, a model of different actors in the system and the information that flowed from one to another, and a model of the laws that had changed to support the current system. The interdisciplinary team had different models from different disciplinary perspectives, so how could it build a shared understanding of what to design? For instance, one team member wanted to focus on how the apathy of citizens was augmenting the problem and how the team could change that apathy. Another team member wanted to focus on spreading awareness about the DWCCs. Team members had different models supporting their understanding, they had different perspectives on these models, but they needed to figure out what they were working toward.

For instance, in the beginning, the team wanted to do "something in the area of urban waste." This was not just a stated intent; it was a well-thought-out plan that was supported by contextual information. It is how each designer in the team had perceived the issue. Eventually, the focus changed to "the newly implemented decentralized system of solid waste in Bangalore, with a particular emphasis on DWCCs." Finally, the team decided to focus on "What we could do to help DWCCs managed by people from the informal sector to make a profit?" Their shared understanding of what to design was built on pieces drawn from different models. It was a story they told together, a narrative they weaved together to explain to themselves and to others what they wanted to design. Their shared understanding of the artifact being designed was an abstraction of the artifact, or a theory of the artifact.

What is a theory? A theory explains a certain phenomenon in a concise manner. It is systematically organized knowledge applicable in a relatively wide variety of circumstances, especially a system of assumptions, accepted principles, and rules of procedure devised to analyze, predict, or explain the nature and behavior of a specified set of phenomena. In general, a theory should answer a variety of questions about the phenomenon it speaks about. A theory of an artifact is thus a contextual theory that provides us with the knowledge for designing and analyzing an artifact. By contextual, we mean that the purview of this theory is limited to a single artifact or a set of artifacts.

The theory of the artifact is a contextual theory that encapsulates knowledge about an artifact that is useful for designing that artifact. It is an interdisciplinary theory consisting of various types of synthetic, analytic, and process knowledge that reconciles many disciplinary theories in the context of the artifact. We as designers not only produce a description of the artifact but also evolve the corresponding theory of the artifact. The theory of the artifact thus harnesses our capacity for abstraction and lets us build on what we have learned. As the process of designing progresses in time, the theory of the artifact changes as well. Thus, the dialogue in designing itself can be viewed as narrating, maintaining, and shaping the theory of the artifact.[14] In a way, the theory of the artifact is an indicator of how robust the dialogue in designing is.

In the case of Fields of View's project, the theory of the artifact was "something that can help the DWCCs make a profit." The theory of the artifact encapsulated all the models from which team members drew their understanding of the problem, the assumptions, and the decisions—all of the tangible and intangible information that pertained to the design process.

The Game Rubbish!

Given the team's new theory of the artifact, it started looking at the challenges DWCCs faced in terms of profitability. A critical challenge was that the citizens, who are producers of waste, did not understand how their actions affected and contributed to the waste chain. The DWCCs were in the middle of the chain and were dependent on the actions of the producers of waste. This meant that the actions of the citizens—such as the segregation of waste—affected the profitability of the DWCCs. Team members wondered what they could do to make citizens understand how their actions affected these middlemen and how dependent they were on these actions. So they decided to build a gaming simulation.

Gaming simulations provide a safe, nonthreatening space for the player to play with a system in an immersive fashion. Players can experience different situations, and in making decisions in the game, they can weigh trade-offs and experience the consequences of their actions. Moreover, the gaming simulation can be built on a model that combines social, economic, and environmental considerations. Therefore, through a gaming simulation, citizens could engage with the waste ecosystem in all its complexity.

The team designed Rubbish! or Kaasu-kasa, a bilingual board game supported in English and Kannada, where citizens could play the role of DWCC managers.[15] In playing the game, citizens could experience firsthand the challenges of managing dry waste, see how hard it was to make a profit in a system where not many people segregated their waste, and understand the complex tug of war between environment, economics, and societal power

Figure 5.1
Rubbish!, the game. Image reprinted with permission from Fields of View.

structures. The goal was to help create more informed citizens, a small step toward creating more conscious citizens.

In the game, players took on the role of DWCC managers, and their activities consisted of buying, sorting, and selling dry waste. The players' goal was to create a center in every ward of the city. Whatever waste the players did not collect went into a landfill. When the landfill was brought to capacity, the game would end, and no one would have won.

The game acted as a space to extend the dialogue on waste between different actors. Although the game did not preach waste segregation, it helped the participants to begin a discussion on how they could segregate better. After having played the game, people better understood the system and also their role in the success of the system.

Since the design of the first prototype, a temporary closure, the game has undergone many changes based on feedback from different sessions and has also been created in Tamil. With more contexts of use and sessions, the game's design will continue to evolve. The game has been and continues to be used by different civil society groups to conduct sessions for citizens. Surprisingly, a school expressed the desire to use the game to teach mathematics to high school students. As it is with designing, the theory of the artifact of the game will continue to change as long as the game lives.

What Is Waste?

Going back to the question we started with, let us think about the afterlife. What happens when someone loved dies?

She was a great-grandmother whose silver hair used to be tied into a bun that looked like an egg spun with shiny threads. She made pickles that were annually distributed to the entire extended family. When she passed away at what is called a ripe old age, the family mourned but also celebrated. In many cultures, the death of a loved one is both mourned and celebrated. Life is seen as cyclical. The old moves on, and the new finds breath.

Imagine that this great-grandmother's porcelain jar is passed on to the next generation. If you receive such a jar from the elders in your family, it is more than a storage device for pickles. There is a relationship you forge with that object, a relationship that is braided with tradition, emotion, stories, and memory. The value of that pickle jar is not just monetary or utilitarian (which is to hold a certain number of pickles), but its value has an ineffable aspect to it. If such a jar breaks, a small piece of your heart would break too.

What happens to the objects we design after they die? As designers who are concerned with making, the afterlife of objects is our concern, too. If an object is valued only for its use, then after its utility fades, it becomes refuse and is thrown onto the rubbish heap. In a culture driven by consumption, when everyone is seen as a user or consumer, then what is deemed as refuse is a function of utility and value. After the utility has been lost, the value vanishes, too. Designing in this case is concerned about how to fuel that consumption, and the consequences of such a design are mountains of rubbish. Perhaps, how we see garbage is at the heart of what it means to design.

If we as designers do not reduce people to users and instead view and work with people as complex beings, such an approach to design would reflect in our relationship with the material and natural world. If every object we create is respectful of the natural world, then our relationship with the natural world that is mediated by these objects will be respectful too. The relationship with a material object would be a relationship that grants meaning to both—the object and our lives—because that is what makes a relationship human.

The Story of Designing So Far

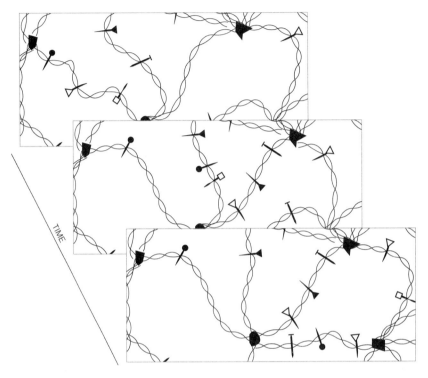

Figure 5.2
The dialogue in designing can be seen as an act of continuous modeling. Temporary closures punctuate the dialogue. The state of the artifact keeps evolving during the dialogue. The theory of the artifact involves a shared understanding of the state of the artifact resides in the models, the artifact being designed, and the people involved in the dialogue.

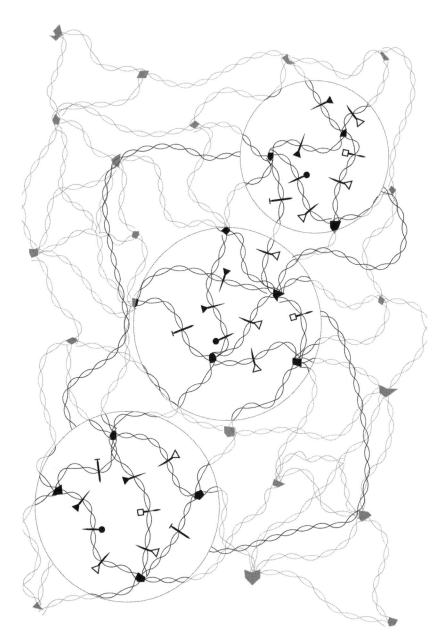

Figure 5.3
The process of designing is a dialogue with other models, artifacts, and perspectives, which are all part of the shared memory—a living repository of the knowledge associated with designing.

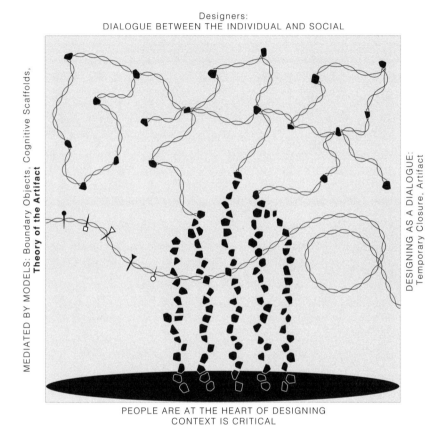

Figure 5.4
Seeing the dialogue in designing as an act of continuous modeling.

6   Context, Context, Context

context

NOUN

1 The circumstances that form the setting for an event, statement, or idea, and in terms of which it can be fully understood. ...

Origin

Late Middle English (denoting the construction of a text): from Latin contextus, from con- 'together' + texere 'to weave.'

—*Oxford English Dictionary*

The Curious Case of Context

Yet again, we wish there were a better word than *context* to speak about context. It seems too tame to describe an idea that is multilayered and exceedingly rich in its implications. At times, words like *situated*, *rooted*, and *local* are used to describe something as being contextual, but none quite manages to encapsulate the myriad levels or scope of the word. For instance, a context can imply a geographical context (such as Sumatra), a disciplinary setting (such as a postcolonial analysis of South Asian literature), or an imagined idea (such as a utopian future). We can say "in the context of" and get away with describing any of these settings, and it would make perfect sense.

Beginning in chapter 2, we have spoken and argued about the importance of context to designing. It is the reason that universal theories of designing remain a wishful dream. It is why what works in Bangkok does not necessarily make sense in Baghdad. In chapter 3, we argue for an approach to design that gives context the critical importance it is due and conceive of designing as a dialogue between the artifact and the context. In chapter 4, we draw on different disciplines and weave together a theoretical base for designing that is situated in the context. And in chapter 5, we elaborate on concepts such as shared memory and designing as a basis for the building of the theory of the artifact and means that help us realize such an approach to designing.

Yet one question remains. So far, we have not tried to unravel the threads that make up context in designing. What are its dimensions, and how do we characterize it? Are there any similarities between different contexts, and if so, how can we deepen our understanding of the different contexts in which designing takes place and learn from those experiences?

Reiterating what we say in chapter 3, the root of the word *context* lies in *con* ("to bring together") and *texere* ("to weave"). It is similar to the word *complex* (*com* + *plectere*, which means "to weave"). Context is complex, and it may not be possible to understand all its interwoven dimensions. What we present here is a starting point.

Over more than two decades of research in designing, we have developed a framework that we use to characterize different contexts in which designing takes place. We call it the PSI (problem, social, institutional) framework.[1] By characterizing the context along three spaces—the problem space,[2] the social space, and the institutional space, which in turn have three axes each—we attempt to understand similarities, delve into differences, and enrich the shared memory of designing.

In order to present the framework, let us travel to Bangalore in September 2013, where a small team at Fields of View, a not-for-profit research organization, set out with the following problem: Given the debate over women's safety in public spaces, can we design options to enhance a sense of security for women in such spaces?[3] The team consisted of students from Bangalore and Amsterdam, and their backgrounds were in information technology and media studies.

We give this story the shape of a table where we clearly separate the details into three categories or spaces.[4] The first space, the problem space, tells us what the problem being addressed is.[5] The second space, the social space, tells us who was involved in the process of designing. And the third space, the institutional space, tells us how those involved in the social space were organized and the processes they undertook to design the product.

For the problem (P) space, we use the following characteristics:

1. Disciplinary complexity: Marks the distinct disciplines (such as mechanical, electrical engineering, and software) that are involved in the design process.

2. Structural complexity: Deals with the number and complexity of issues and their interconnections.

3. Knowledge availability: Ranges from knowledge readily available (known) in principle to knowledge that needs to be generated through research and experimentation.

For the social (S) space, we use the following characteristics:

1. Number of perspectives: Deals with the different perspectives participants bring to the table, where perspectives could be interpreted broadly not only as a point of view but also as a disciplinary perspective (such as that of an engineer, a marketing person, or a maintenance person).

2. Inclusion: Takes a range between closed (only members of a closed group are involved) and open (members external to the team are invited to participate, as in an open source effort).

3. Capabilities and skills: Refers to the capabilities and skills of those involved in the design (such as creative thinking, systems thinking, analytical skills, disciplinary knowledge of methods and theories, and practical knowledge).

For the institutional (I) space, we have three characteristics:

1. Ties: Refers to the strength of interconnections (strong and weak) between entities involved in designing.[6]

2. Knowledge accessibility: Deals with the awareness of existence of knowledge (formal and informal) and the mechanisms to share among the participants in designing.[7]

3. Institutional structures: Characterizes the routines, communication patterns, rules, procedures, tools, and culture of those involved in the design.[8]

All these spaces and their characteristics are intricate, allowing for multiple interpretations. The dimensions that characterize the spaces are about the individual entities that make up the dimension (such as number of disciplines) and also the interconnections among them.

Coming back to the team in Bangalore, the initial idea was to build a panic button to address the issue of women's safety in public spaces. What the team had in mind was something that could be worn as a bracelet or necklace that could be activated in times of emergencies. It made sense to the team to create a panic button to address the problem because team members had the knowledge required to build the panic button, and it seemed meaningful as well as useful. The team baptized the project as the Unpanic Button Project, for the idea was that the button should help the woman to "unpanic."

When a sociologist who also specialized in gender studies joined the team as an adviser, the entire frame of the problem changed. From a position of knowing about the problem and ways to design for it, team members found that they had to learn and understand the problem better. The team jettisoned the idea of designing a panic button and began examining the problem afresh, which led to three different ideas, out of which one was chosen and designed.

We will elaborate on the team's journey through the PSI framework. As mentioned earlier, initially the idea was to create a panic button to address the issue of safety of women in public spaces. The team had all the required information and skills necessary to design the panic button. The initial state of the project as described in the PSI spaces is shown in the table below.

Design context: Designing a panic button to address the safety of women in public spaces in Bangalore

---

Problem space (WHAT problem is being addressed?)

Disciplinary complexity	Low: It requires only technology and engineering disciplines.
Structural complexity	Low: The design of a panic button is simple.
Knowledge availability	Complete: All the knowledge required to design the panic button is available.

Social space (WHO designs?)

Number of perspectives	One: That of students who share a similar socioeconomic background and exposure to the issue

---

Inclusion	Limited
Capabilities and skills	Technology, media and culture studies, including all knowledge needed to design the product

Institutional space (HOW?)	

Ties	Strong
Knowledge accessibility	Knowledge is accessible to all participants.
Institutional structures	An informal way of operating

Reframing the Problem

This was the time a sociologist, who specialized in women's studies and had worked for several years as a counselor for victims of rape and sexual assault, joined the team. She was not happy with the project's name, the Unpanic Button Project.

According to her, the word *unpanic* came from the same frame of mind that considered women as hysterical and emotional beings who are incapable of rationality: "In fact, if we are telling women NOT to panic, we are telling women two things—one, that they do panic (which they do not) and that they ought not to panic (why not when the fear is real enough)."

The sociologist provoked the team to think more about what it means to ask for the safety of women in public places. For instance, would asking women to stay at home after dark be acceptable as a design option if your aim is the safety of women? The ongoing dialogue with the sociologist made team members dig deeper into the implications of what their aim ought to be. They found that the framing of the problem was in line with that of a patriarchal society that seeks to protect its women. In such a framework, women are equivalent to property that needs to be protected rather than self-actualizing beings.

In the aftermath of the rape of a young woman in the Indian capital in December 2012, a committee was created under Justice Verma to examine the existing laws around sexual assault. This progressive committee framed its focus not as the safety of women but as women's autonomy, thereby ensuring that women's freedom did not become hostage to safety.

The sociologist introduced the book *Why Loiter? Women and Risk on Mumbai Streets* by Shilpa Phadke, Sameera Khan, and Shilpa Ranade.[9] In the book, the authors provocatively argue that loitering in public spaces is discomfiting for Indian women. They go out with a purpose, never to loiter. And the idea of loitering—claiming public spaces as your own and enjoying freedom and independence in the public space coupled with the idea of risk—is the central theme of the book.

Inspired by the book and other readings and discussions with the sociologist, the team shifted its focus from women's safety to women's autonomy and freedom in the public space. The change in focus also brought the designing of the panic button into question: was the wearable panic button still a viable design option under the new goal, which was to work toward the freedom and autonomy of women in public spaces in India?[10]

The team began digging further to understand the nature of the problem women face in public spaces in India and critique the design of the panic button under the lens of gender theory.

The debate around women's safety in public spaces in India had led to the development of a lot of panic buttons and SOS applications on mobile phones. The team originally wanted to create a wearable panic button, continuing with the same reasoning that led to the design of these other panic buttons and SOS devices. When team members examined the shared memory related to the panic buttons and SOS applications, they realized that it did not include insights and learning from gender theory and studies on women's experiences in public spaces. For instance, in different surveys women have uniformly indicated that bystander help is never available and that bystanders sometimes join in the harassment. If this insight was taken into account, then the design of devices that alert bystanders nearby of an incident of harassment could turn the situation potentially more harmful.

The sociologist reiterated the need to expand the shared memory of artifacts to include the lived experiences of women: "Any design of technology must put women's lived experiences at the center for the intervention of technologies." By asking women to carry a panic button, the onus of safety was once again on the women themselves, which belonged in the same frame as holding women responsible for anything that happened to them. This blamed the victim instead of the perpetrator: Why did you go out at night? Why did you wear that? Why did you not carry your panic button?

At this juncture, the team decided to drop the idea of creating a panic button and to explore the problem afresh.

We see that initially, the limited social space of the team had led it to formulate the problem, as well as the design, in a narrow technical sense (the designing of a panic button), which they could address comfortably. It marked a misalignment between the S space and the broader social, cultural, economic context—a misalignment between the complex problem at hand or P space, and the team's limited knowledge and capabilities.[11] Such a misalignment is a common problem termed *collective tunnel vision* or *groupthink*[12] and translates into solutions that are possible within the scope of the capabilities of the team rather than the understanding of the problem itself. The dialogue with the sociologist mitigated the collective tunnel vision, reinforcing the need for as many diverse perspectives as possible to understand the problem better in order to move toward a better design.

The resulting description in the PSI spaces was as follows:

Design context: Freedom and autonomy of women in public spaces in Bangalore	
Problem space (WHAT?)	
Disciplinary complexity	Unknown
Structural complexity	Unknown
Knowledge availability	Unknown
Social space (WHO?)	
Number of perspectives	Two: That of students who share a similar socioeconomic background and exposure to the issue and a sociologist who was an expert on gender issues
Inclusion	More open
Capabilities and skills	Technological, media and culture, gender theory, and sociology
Institutional space (HOW?)	
Ties	Strong
Knowledge accessibility	Knowledge is accessible to all participants.
Institutional structures	Informal way of operating

Digging Further and Three Problem Formulations

The team members began to further their understanding of the nature of women's lived experiences when it came to public spaces in India. One of the questions they started out with was, "What is the nature of rape in India?"

The team found that according to statistics, "the overwhelming story of rape in India is that of men assaulting girls and women they know."[13] A news article that analyzed national crime statistics goes on to say, "The sort of cases that hit the headlines are usually those in which the offense was committed by a stranger. It's instructive to see from these numbers how such cases, though undoubtedly heinous, do not reflect the broader nature of rape in India." This implies that most cases of rape in India are not by anonymous strangers, as horrendous as such cases are, but by people known to the victim.

Given the focus on issues women faced in public spaces, the team turned its attention to sexual harassment. To understand more about the nature of sexual harassment in India and the types of interventions that might be possible, the team interviewed different experts in the field, including the founder of a women's rights organization in the city, a veteran journalist who covers gender issues, and members of a women's rights organization that has worked on issues of gender justice for over two decades. These interviews reinforced the view that sexual harassment in public spaces was a layered and complex problem with many dimensions.

The context thus shifted from a well-defined technical problem driven by one perspective into a broader, somewhat unknown challenge resulting from expanding perspectives in the social space. It was clear that without openness to and inclusion of other perspectives, the social space would be compromised, and the PSI would be misaligned again.

The team created various models to understand the varied dimensions of the issue, including visuals depicting relationships between different actors and institutions, as well as reports on different aspects of the issue. These models mediated the process of designing and helped team members arrive at a shared understanding of the path they charted.

Using these models, the team analyzed the issue of sexual harassment and decided to focus on three related issues—the culture of masculinity, the need for a resource base of different initiatives dedicated to women's freedom and mobility, and a lack of data on street sexual harassment.

The project dealing with the culture of masculinity was marked for the future (temporary closure) because the required number of perspectives was not accessible immediately and the duration of the project was only five months (time constraints).

As can be seen in the table below, the project focusing on the culture of masculinity had a misalignment of PSI spaces that called for an action (limiting the scope) to create a project with aligned and meaningful PSI spaces. Given the time constraints, a project that was related to a resource base of different initiatives dedicated to women's freedom and mobility was also marked for the future.[14]

The analysis of the PSI spaces of the project on the culture of masculinity, which indicates an issue in the social spaces, is given in the following table:

Design context: Freedom and autonomy of women in public spaces in Bangalore—A culture of masculinity	
Problem space (WHAT?)	
Disciplinary complexity	Very high
Structural complexity	Unknown
Knowledge availability	Not fully available with the new institutional structure
Social space (WHO?)	
Number of perspectives	Several: Students who share a similar socioeconomic background and exposure to the issue, a sociologist who is an expert on gender issues, the founder of a women's rights organization, a veteran journalist, and members of a women's rights organization
Inclusion	More openness and inclusion of new perspectives
Capabilities and skills	Analytical, sociological, policy advocacy, gender issues, practitioners in the field of fighting against sexual violence An analysis of the social space shows that the team lacks access to an expert on gender issues with a focus on masculinity and a psychologist focusing on masculinity.

Institutional space (HOW?)	
Ties	The creation of new ties with other perspectives both weak through literature and strong through personal interactions
Knowledge accessibility	Improved accessibility to knowledge about the problem through new dialogues and interactions
Institutional structures	Beyond a small group to a network of organizations and people

Breaking the Silence around Sexual Harassment

The team chose to focus on the lack of actionable data on sexual harassment, which rendered the issue invisible. Moreover, the lack of data makes it difficult to advocate for policy change or design meaningful programs and products to address the issue. In other words, the shared memory of any design intervention to address the issue of women's freedom in public spaces would need this data. Thus, the team's goal was to design a way to collect data on street sexual harassment, which formed the theory of the artifact.

Different concepts were created, including a campaign where women would be given a flowering plant that could be planted at the site of the harassment, an ironic way to show the areas where more incidents of harassment occurred. Another concept was to share what happened over a cup of coffee, where the number of coffee cups collected in the bin would tell the story of harassment. There were ideas to create a narrative around characters that would encourage women to come forward with their experiences. The team created models and visuals of these different concepts, which would mediate the dialogue between the team and the experts and help decide how to proceed.

Figure 6.1 shows the visual models that were created to illustrate the flowering plant campaign and the cup of coffee campaign described earlier.

After debating various such ideas, using visual models as mediators, the team decided to build a kiosk that could be installed in public spaces, somewhat like an ATM machine, where women could informally report cases of street sexual harassment. The process of refining the theory of the artifact (in this case, the kiosk) continued.

CONCEPTS

1. Campaign

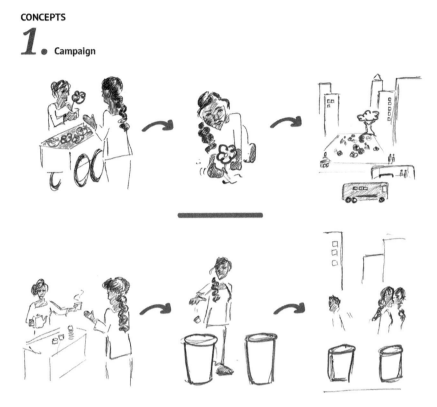

Figure 6.1
Sketches of concepts: 1. Image reprinted with permission from Fields of View.

The visual in figure 6.2 shows initial sketches of the concept of what the kiosk could do. It could potentially contain a screen that would let the woman enter details of what happened, as well as a phone that could connect to a helpline. The data collected could be displayed on a public screen (image in the center).

A kiosk in a physical space was chosen over a web-based application because of certain key insights obtained during discussions between team members and different experts and practitioners. The experts from the women's rights group told the team that any digital platform (web or smartphone) to report on cases of sexual harassment would not be accessible to a large number of women because smartphone penetration in India is not high. The use of smartphones would exclude many people from weaker economic sections.

2. Panel

Screen   Phone

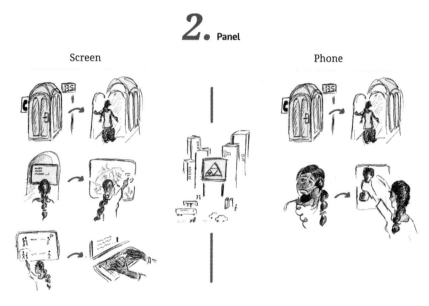

Figure 6.2
Sketches of concepts: 2. Image reprinted with permission from Fields of View.

Because one of the key requirements was to reach women from different strata of society, the kiosk had to support multiple languages and allow women who were not conversant with technology and different levels of literacy to access the device. In order to further refine the theory of the artifact to include knowledge on how to make the device more accessible to women of different economic strata with different kinds of literacies, the team spoke to an interface designer who specialized in creating interfaces for people with different kinds of literacies. Her work shows that an interface that is a combination of audio and visual directions works for people who do not have verbal literacy.[15] In addition, in the Indian context, abstract symbols do not work. Therefore, pictograms, which are not as noisy as photographs and not at the level of abstraction as symbols, were required. The team then created an interface that was audiovisual in nature and contained pictograms and an audio layer supporting multiple languages.

The kiosk that the team created was called Convers[t]ation, a way to break silences around sexual harassment. The theory of the artifact, Convers[t]ation, includes the technical and functional aspects of its design (technology such as the kind of monitor used, the processor, the software,

An artist's impression of Convers[t]ation in a bus station.

Figure 6.3
An artist's rendition of Convers[t]ation. Image reprinted with permission from Fields of View. *Source:* Fields of View, "White Paper Documenting the Process of Designing Convers[t]ation," 2014, http://fieldsofview.in/publications/visuals/WhitePaper Converstation2014.

and the hardware, as well as multilingual and audiovisual support) and also the institutional framework required for it to be effective. The institutional framework involves sharing data among citizens, civil society groups, and the government. This institutional connect among these three groups was crucial for the success of Convers[t]ation.

The description of the last step in the evolution of the project is shown in the next table. These descriptions evolved significantly from the first conception of the Unpanic Button. Such a trajectory in the PSI spaces is expected in any project.

Design context: Freedom and autonomy of women in public spaces in Bangalore—Kiosk for informally reporting cases of sexual harassment	
Problem space (WHAT?)	
Disciplinary complexity	Sufficient for the design of the kiosk Disciplinary complexity is not adequate for wide-scale implementation in the city (for example, because of governance issues and institutionalization issues).

Structural complexity	Moderate level for the kiosk design but not in terms of consistent service and use at the sites
Knowledge availability	Technical knowledge available for kiosk design

Social space (WHO?)	
Number of perspectives	Students who share a similar socioeconomic background and exposure to the issue, a sociologist who is an expert on gender issues, the founder of a women's rights organization, a veteran journalist, members of a women's rights organization, and an expert on user interfaces The number of perspectives would require additional organizations in the network for implementation in the city.
Inclusion	More open
Capabilities and skills	Analytical, computing, user interface design, sociological, policy advocacy, gender issues, and practitioners in the field of fighting against sexual violence

Institutional space (HOW?)	
Ties	Strong ties were established with different participants and institutions.
Knowledge accessibility	Sufficient Knowledge availability was incomplete due to the need to connect to institutional structures.
Institutional structures	A partial network structure with the design team and other organizations representing the perspectives and disciplines

Convers[t]ation is now being prototyped and tested in Bangalore, and different institutional frameworks are being explored. The team achieved a temporary closure in terms of designing the kiosk. The next phase of designing will involve the institutional connect—how the local transport agency, the women's rights organization, and citizens communicate with each other and what processes are in place to act on the data collected through the device. The arena of designing shifts to these different formal and informal institutions, the social space changes, and the problem and the institutional space change accordingly.

Meanwhile, the ambit of the kiosk has been widened to include not just women but anyone who wishes to report cases of sexual harassment. More tests are being done to understand this changed social space and see how it affects the design of the kiosk (the problem and the institutional space). In addition, different contexts of use are being explored to report cases of sexual harassment from washrooms at workplaces and college campuses.

Transformers Revisited

Let us now shift our focus to the case of the transformer company that we discuss in chapter 4 to see how the problem space, social space, and institutional space (PSI) framework helps characterize and negotiate a completely different context—a corporate design setting.

Power transformers are integral to the operation of electric power systems. One transformer company began as a local producer and supplier and expanded to become a global producer and supplier of the product. To achieve this goal, the company bought transformer companies in several countries.

Each of these companies had its own knowledge base of design and product and its own understanding of the needs of the market. In effect, each had its own shared memory of the product in terms of methods, models, people, and organizations of the design and manufacturing process. Each also had a theory of the artifact embedded in its organizational shared memory. In effect, these companies had the problem space, social space, and institutional space aligned to serve their local markets.

However, in its quest for globalization, the transformer company had to leverage the economies of scale by integrating these different companies in various countries. It planned to integrate the different companies by creating a common product structure that could accommodate the variations of different markets. In other words, a new shared memory and theory of the artifact had to be created to deal with local demands using global resources.

PSI: Initial State

Initially, the PSI of the parent power transformer company was well defined and aligned over its long history, reflecting a company with proven capabilities over decades of operation.

Design context: Transformation from local to global	
Problem space (WHAT?)	
Disciplinary complexity	Complex as reflected by this electromechanical infrastructure product—electrical, mechanical, marketing and maintenance
Structural complexity	Medium complexity
Knowledge availability	A classic product with specific available know-how of the technology, markets, and needs; the continuous encoding of the theory of the artifact
Social space (WHO?)	
Number of perspectives	Sufficient for this complex product but related to a particular market
Inclusion	Limited to the knowledge of the local customers and the disciplinary skills needed
Capabilities and skills	All the required skills and capabilities for a successful practice
Institutional space (HOW?)	
Ties	Very strong ties within the company and with customers
Knowledge accessibility	Easily accessible due to both locational and strong ties within and across functional boundaries
Institutional structures	Routines, rules, and processes well established; rotation of employees across divisional boundaries; well-defined interfaces

The Challenge of Globalization

What changes to the PSI (problem, social, institutional) spaces were needed to complete the journey from being a local player to a global one? One important change was to move the company's mainly paper-based mechanisms for managing knowledge to a computer-based mechanism that would support distributed work. This required adding external expertise to support the process and was the impetus to bring into the process the n-dim group (described in appendix B). The table on following page illustrates these challenges.

Design context: Transformer company from local to global	
Problem space (WHAT?)	
Disciplinary complexity	Disciplinary complexity increases not from core technical disciplines but from a managerial and marketing perspective.
Structural complexity	Structural complexity increases due to the different compositional structures required due to different manufacturing practices.
Knowledge availability	A classic product with specific available know-how; other knowledge is only partially known because the availability of knowledge is not charted within each of the merged companies There is a need for new shared memory and theory of the artifact.
Social space (WHO?)	
Number of perspectives	Differential design processes The number of perspectives needs to increase based on the increased variety of customers.
Inclusion	From limited to broader global inclusion of perspectives from customers, marketing, and technology approaches
Capabilities and skills	Even: They share a common base of technological goals and the function of the product, capability, and skill-base variations.
Institutional space (HOW?)	
Ties	Classic: They require radical changes in creating new ties across the merged companies at different levels of organizations and functions.
Knowledge accessibility	As determined by company procedures: Procedures, rules, routing embedded in people, and paper documents Knowledge accessibility needs to be radically restructured for accessibility of knowledge and accumulation. Need for creating and maintaining new shared memory and modes for accessibility.
Institutional structures	A traditional business: There is not a single firm with supplier network but a global network of design, manufacturing and supplier network structures. There is a need for new routines, roles, and communication patterns.

The company had to create ways to share knowledge across the acquired companies and balance design and production resources. Therefore, knowledge accessibility had to become easy. Institutional structures had to be changed to allow for resources from one company to be available to another. For this to happen, the company had to pay attention to the commonalities and differences between different products (a P space consideration) to make knowledge transfer possible (an I space consideration).

Globalization could be achieved only by harmonizing the product across markets. Harmonizing implied creating a new product structure (affecting the P space). This meant there had to be new models of different physical, geometrical, and production aspects of the product (such as calculating insulation and heat transfer needs, computing the electromagnetic flux, optimizing properties and sizing of transformers, describing geometric product dimensions, and creating organizational models for design and manufacture across different locations).

The acquired companies had these models, but they used different tools and variants of methods for their design and production. The need now was to harmonize models, tools, and production processes. In effect, a new theory of the artifact that could account for variety had to be constructed, which would in turn provide substrate (data, experience, theory, models) for the company to build a new shared memory of the transformer and attendant practices.

The Journey to Globalization

To create a new theory of the artifact, the company created a team that included people (such as R&D managers, production managers, and marketing managers) from the different merged companies. The team also recruited people from academia. This resulted in a change in the S space.

The team created new shared product structure models, including computer-aided tools that modeled the physics of the transformer using collective empirical data from the acquired companies. A new design environment was created that captured the shared memory as the design progressed. Having this design environment meant that the theory of the artifact and attendant models could be continuously updated and captured in the shared memory.

In other words, the move into a merged company involved aligning the individual PSI spaces of the acquired companies into a single one. It is a recursive process, as any act of designing is. A team of company professionals and external experts (S) was assembled and charted by the management and through a contract (I) (a combination we call PSI at the alignment level) to change the situation of the company (S) and its operation and tools (I) so it could approach the stage where it could develop better products (P).

Design context: A global company operating in multiple locations	
Problem space (WHAT?): Now the product is the new organization (and its PSI).	
Disciplinary complexity	Knowledge about organization structuring, managing variety, and information; more complex than before to include systems
Structural complexity	As before, compounded by variety
Knowledge availability	Available internally about product and externally about streamlining organizational processes within the external R&D
Social space (WHO?)	
Number of perspectives	People from different companies with different perspectives (such as R&D and production) plus external team of researchers (Carnegie Mellon University n-dim group)
Inclusion	Limited but all necessary
Capabilities and skills	Necessary to understand the problems arising from variety
Institutional space (HOW?)	
Ties	Small group interaction plus a relation to an external R&D group
Knowledge accessibility	Accessible to team members with selective access to external R&D team
Institutional structures	Evolving set of routines and practices plus a contract with an external R&D team

Using the PSI Model

A dialogue eludes prescription. Meaning, thought, creativity: these emerge from the dialogue, which is designing. Therefore, our focus is on the dialogue itself—how it takes place, what the conditions in which it takes place are, and what insights we can bring to examine those conditions. Our attempt in building a vocabulary to describe this dialogue in designing is to enable such an examination, and in this section, we ask some questions that we hope will help in probing the dialogue in designing.

Who?

Who are the people participating in designing? It is a question of diversity. Are there enough perspectives on board to address the complexities of what is being designed? For instance, during the design of Convers[t]ation, after it was decided that a kiosk should be created, the team required the expertise of an interface designer. The design process benefits from constant questioning. How can more perspectives be invited to participate? How can we increase diversity? The dimensions of the S space help in understanding and examining the diversity of perspectives.

How and What?

Designing is about not just the artifact being designed but also the process of designing, the dialogue. With the dialogue in designing, it is a question of paying attention to the models. For starters, what kind of boundary objects are being used? Can more meaningful boundary objects be designed such that the dialogue is deeper? How is the shared memory being maintained?

The theory of the artifact is for us the measure of the health of the process of designing.[16] It shows you how robust the boundary objects and the cognitive scaffolds they rest on are and how well maintained the shared memory is. Thus, for us, designing is about constantly paying attention to the creation and maintenance of the theory of the artifact.

The problem, social, and institutional spaces provide insights into the state of the theory of the artifact. They tell us about the complexity of the artifact being designed, the interfaces that require boundary objects, the necessary capabilities and expertise for designing, and the procedures, culture, and rules of the designing organization. The PSI spaces thus provide us with insights into how the dialogue between designers, artifact, and the context unfolds and also help us negotiate the dialogue.

Once again, these different aspects of designing—the who, what, and the how (and therefore the P space, S space, and I space)—are in a dialogue with each other. They cannot be considered in isolation. Rather, they inform and shape each other during the dialogue of designing.

Our goal is to build the shared memory of designing by characterizing different contexts in which designing takes place using the PSI framework. For instance, we could have walked through any one of the stories told in this book (whether the House of Nine Muses, the *agarbattis* project, the production of *Samhara,* or the book itself) and described its context in PSI to explain its successes and hurdles and help in its future development. Such an analysis would become an intrinsic part of the story. Our ongoing research involves deepening this structure to describe and distinguish between different contexts. Such distinctions will allow designers to better fit their design processes to the context.

As we study more designing contexts, we hope to discover patterns that will tell us which design situations are similar to one another and which in turn will help us characterize classes of different design contexts. In this way, the PSI framework not only helps characterize designing contexts but also becomes a decision-making tool for carrying the design process forward. As such, it introduces again the recursive nature of designing. With all these and other planned developments in the PSI framework, the PSI model as it stands today, like any other artifact, is a temporary closure.

The Story of Designing So Far

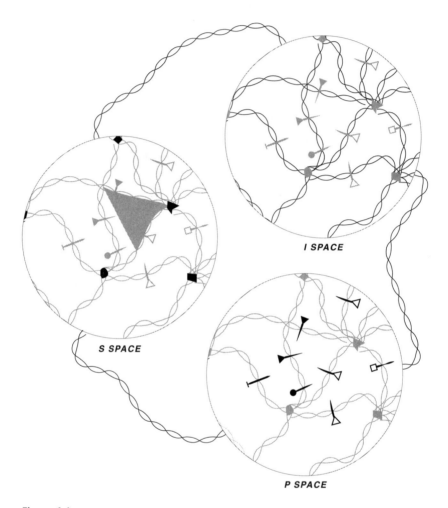

Figure 6.4

The dialogue is a context-dependent process. We use the PSI framework to characterize and provide insights into the context. The P space gives you insights on what problem is being addressed. The S space gives you insights into who designs. And the I space gives you insights on the state of the dialogue or the how.

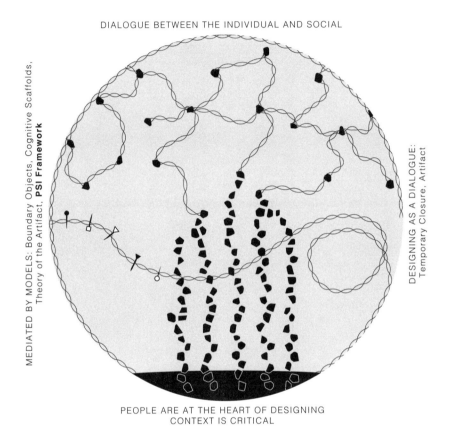

Figure 6.5
Our contribution to the shared memory of designing.

7   Designing Our Future

Where roads are made I lose my way.
In the wide water, in the blue sky there is no line of a track.
The pathway is hidden by the birds' wings, by the star-fires, by the flowers of the wayfaring seasons.
And I ask my heart if its blood carries the wisdom of the unseen way.

—Rabindranath Tagore, "Poem VI," *Fruit Gathering*

Dialogue

This last chapter is about pausing, drawing a breath, and looking back at the path we have traversed. We started by journeying through a short summary of how designing had been studied throughout the ages and examined questions that arose out of that extensive romp through history. We then teased out a vocabulary that questioned the fixedness of parts and wholes and is built on the dialogue between them. We drew on cognitive science, linguistic theories, ethnographic studies, and other empirical evidence to build our case. We outlined the conception of a dialogue in all its richness. We then tried to understand designing as a dialogue that develops in time and the importance of context and collaboration in that dialogue. We ended up with the critical value that dialogue requires—diversity. We then looked at the space in which this dialogue takes place and constructed the stage in which the dance of design unfolds.

Now what? It is tempting to end with to-do lists, grand plans to change the world, and promises of a better tomorrow. If we do this, this, and this, then we will design the world our ancestors could only dream of. This approach is very tempting. We see crisis after crisis: a planet that will soon house 10 billion people is a cauldron for all sorts of problems. And we do believe that designing offers us insights into negotiating this minefield. But if we did give you maps of how we could alter our lives and our planet on the basis of what we have said so far, we would have stopped the dialogue even before it began. And that is the trap we have been doing our best to avoid—having a fixed view of the world.

Right from birth, we are indoctrinated to think in fixed terms. Take the question "What do you want to be when you grow up?" It is a question most of us had to answer as children. No matter what our response to the question—railway engine driver, postwoman, teacher, fireman, brain surgeon, politician, or doctor—we love to think about the future and imagine what it will be like. This way of thinking sticks. Most politicians talk about congestion-free roads, a corruption-free country, zero unemployment, pollution-free cities, and a hunger-free world. Many doctors wonder about a disease-free world. Some tired hearts dream of a utopia.

In all these cases, the future is an object, a state to be achieved, an end in itself. It is fixed. We do not see ourselves as an evolving entity or as a being that can change with time. We box ourselves in regard to others, and we envision our collective futures.

Instead of stagnating at a point, what if we think of the future as continuous—as an unfolding story whose next chapter is a few unturned pages away or as another step toward an unseen path? What if we think of a future as a process? The value of dialogue is that it allows us to conceive of the future as a dynamic and changeable state.

Consider this: there is a conflict taking place a few thousand kilometers away. Two countries are at war. We sit in our comfortable drawing rooms, speculating about the war. We have firm ideas about what should be done. Some say force is the only answer. Others say the conflict should continue until it wears out everyone. Some others advocate peace at all costs. What such presumptions let you avoid is the need for a dialogue. A dialogue is not just a conversation. A dialogue is an attempt to be open, to listen, and to have a willingness to be persuaded. It could take a long time. It could shake beliefs that you hold dear.

A new journalist may go to the field with fixed ideas about the story she has to report on. She may have decided that the government is corrupt and is doing nothing to improve health conditions in the state. But when she starts speaking to government officials, she realizes their point of view, their constraints, their issues, and their problems. What she has is a richer understanding of the problem, one that is far removed from her original assumption. But unless she has an open mind, such an understanding will evade her.

And that's what a dialogue demands—an open mind and a willingness to engage with respect. If we want a dialogue, we need to start by creating spaces for such a dialogue to take place. These are spaces where people can interact with each other and with institutions in an open and respectful fashion.

But all around us broken dialogues litter the world. A public hearing where people air their grievances but where the government ignores what it hears is a broken dialogue. Laws so abstruse that no one can make sense of them are a broken dialogue. Some other instances of broken dialogues include living spaces so alienating that people who live there find no relationship between them and the space around, gadgets and applications that form the detritus of wasted effort and resources, plans and projects that make no sense to the people they are meant for, and meetings to negotiate peace where the minds are fixed and closed. Whether between people, between people and artifacts, or between people and institutions, dialogues have attenuated to one-sided sighs that echo all around us.

But is what we are calling for even possible? If you go about talking to everyone, you will never get anything done. Who has the time to create a dialogue with everyone on the table? What about power structures? Are you so naïve to believe that such dialogues will be allowed?

We answer these questions in two parts. First, the skepticism is understandable. A dialogue does not guarantee that you will see the light at the end of the tunnel. A dialogue opens up the tunnel, it is up to us how we negotiate it. And that is the difficulty of the unseen way. If someone asks us the question "What will the future be like?," we cannot resort to adjectives for there is no noun there. Rather, we see the future as a verb—a collective verb, so to speak. And this collective verb is linked to what we have been speaking of thus far—designing. Designing is about charting the unseen way, and our theories and research are a small step in learning the wisdom of that way.

Designing

Skepticism is based on assumptions and presumptions. Saying the future can be designed reflects a certain philosophical and moral stance. We are saying that the future is not something that we have no say over, something like Saturn's satellites. Rather, the future is of our own making. This implies there is nothing obvious about how the future will pan out. We can change it. The agency can be in our hands. We say that this is possible because at the moment it is as though we assume that institutions and ideologies are like the earth's sediment, formed over millennia, a given fact of our lives. But that is not the case. As philosopher Roberto Mangabeira Unger says in his book *The Self Awakened: Pragmatism Unbound,*

> Institutions and ideologies are not like natural objects, forcing themselves on our consciousness with insistent force and reminding us that we have been born into a world that is not our own. They are nothing but frozen will and interrupted conflict: the residue crystallized out of the suspension or containment of our struggles.[1]

If symbols, artifacts, systems, and environments are human-made, are an act of designing, then they can be altered, changed, and therefore designed or redesigned. A frozen will and an interrupted conflict are utterly human, changeable, and therefore subject to being designed. Unger's philosophy is termed *radical pragmatism* because it is so. We are talking about designing everything around us. It is simple if you think of it. If humans have designed things a certain way, we can alter them too. But some people design systems of power to have a veneer of naturalness about them: it is the way it is, it has always been this way, and it can never change. These statements seem silly if we realize and internalize a simple idea: everything around us is an act of design.

But it is not that simple, is it? Take social hierarchies, for instance. It is the way it is, it has always been this way, and it can never change. But is it really so? Consider this example. In a cooking competition, a team has to finish a few tasks such as milking a goat and making an omelet by hopping from farm to farm in two cars. Quickly, the team members decide that one car will lead, and the other will follow. This is a hierarchy. When the lead car gets lost, the people in the second car decide they needed to take over. They tell the folks in the first car about this change in strategy, and now their positions are reversed. The hierarchy has changed. But social hierarchies are made to seem natural for a reason: "any scheme of rigid social ranks and roles depends, for its perpetuation, on the naturalization or the sanctification of the arrangements that reproduce it."[2] If you think it is natural, you will not question it, and you will not think it needs to be changed or that you can change it. But we can design it because everything around us is an act of design. This idea is, as Unger says, "a requirement for the liberation of the individual from a strongly rooted hierarchy and division."[3] We cannot be free if we do not realize this simple idea: we are the ones who have fashioned the chains that bind us.

Our work is an attempt to forge the language that will help us understand these chains and free ourselves from them. But creating a new language is not an easy task, especially when we are steeped in the old ways of thinking. During discussions about the book, our friends have surprised us by asking us to change certain visuals to include time. Although we speak about the importance of time in thinking about theories, we ourselves are trained to think about theories in a way that does not involve time. The Slovenian philosopher Slavoj Žižek quotes an old Eastern European joke to illustrate the exquisite difficulty of articulating a new language.[4] An East German worker is transferred to Siberia and tells his German friends that he will write letters in code so that the censors can't decipher them. The code is that letters in blue ink are true and letters in red ink are not. After some time, the friend gets a letter written in blue. It says that everything is wonderful. Stores are full of good food. Movie theaters show good films from the West. Apartments are large and luxurious. The only thing you cannot get is red ink.[5] Žižek goes on to then say that "we 'feel free' because we lack the very language to articulate our unfreedom."[6]

Creating a new language is liberating. In his book *Pedagogy of the Oppressed*,[7] educator and philosopher Paulo Freire calls for a dialogical process of education for self-awareness so that people can be freed from being merely passive objects responding to uncontrollable change. Such a dialogical form of education would allow every individual to name the world in his or her own terms.

A dialogue is not easy. *Designing* and *freedom* are beautiful and difficult words. They hint at a grand thought, at possibilities, at a richness that seems saturated within those few syllables. But we can get stuck with a diluted version, a hollowed substitute of these words, when we miss the connection between designing and diversity.

Diversity

If every object is human-made and if every object or action is an act of design, then the implication is that there is no one conception of the future. There is no one or only way—the way it always was, the way it always is, and the way it always will be. There are at least as many ways as there are people involved in the design. Each and every one of us is a designer. Each and every one of us has a responsibility to our collective future. Because we are all guardians at the gates of the possible, we all need to participate in designing this future. Without that diversity of thought and action, we will fall back to a monolithic notion of what designing is and what freedom can mean and a future that is preordained.

Our intent is not to say everyone should be an engineer, a social scientist, a doctor, and a gardener all rolled into one but to underscore that design is a means toward an end and that the end is what affects you. The end could be defined in terms of freedom, choice, morals, and values. And you need to participate in it to decide what it implies and means.

In a 2017 TED Talk, the Nigerian author Chimamanda Ngozi Adichie speaks about "the danger of a single story."[8] When she was growing up in eastern Nigeria, she read British and American children's books where the characters were "white and blue-eyed, they played in the snow, they ate apples, and they talked a lot about the weather, how lovely it was that the sun had come out." These stories, she says, stirred her imagination, and she wrote stories about such characters because her young mind was convinced that stories could not be inhabited by people who ate mangoes, did not play in the snow, and never talked about the weather because they did not have to. Her roommate in the United States was surprised that she could speak English well and that the official language of Nigeria was English. Both Adichie and her roommate drew on a single story that precluded other possibilities, stanched potential, and led them to see the world in only one way, making us all the more poorer for that. It is a single story that is our true poverty.

But diversity is difficult to embrace. It is easier to stand on the mountaintop and with one sweeping gaze flatten everything around us. But if we climb down and roam the valley below, a world of incredible richness awaits. As the entomologist E. O. Wilson puts it,

Bacteria, protistans, nematodes, mites, and other minute creatures swarm around us, an animate matrix that binds Earth's surface. They are objects of potentially endless study and admiration, if we are willing to sweep our vision down from the world lined by the horizon to include the world an arm's length away. A lifetime can be spent in a Magellanic voyage around the trunk of a tree.[9]

A Temporary Closure

If we look at the future as a process, a constant discovery of a way unseen, then this process does not stagnate in a utopia. A utopia implies a definite end, a closure, a well-defined signpost that marks the culmination of a journey. Rather, we view any act of designing as continuous, punctuated by temporary closures.

Can we conceive of such a future together? What we have attempted to show in this book is that a dialogue in diversity in order to design is not just necessary but possible. We do not believe it is easy to do so. An understanding of the context will show us that it is not. There is history, there are entrenched ideas, and power structures can make such change difficult. Is such a conception of a future even possible?

With this book, we are asking a different question: Have we gone far enough? Can we take a few more steps?

It is easier to stick to one story, it is easier to let the situation be, it is easier for us not to embrace the prickly complexity that is an inevitable outcome of diversity. But do we want to be like the old man in the folktale who was searching for something under a streetlight? A passerby asked him. "What are you searching for?" The old man said, "I've dropped my key." The passerby tried looking under the streetlight with him for a while. Then he asked the old man, "Do you remember where you dropped it?" The old man said, "Inside my house." "Then why don't you look there?" asked the outraged passerby. "Because there is no light there!" was the old man's response.

We are not dreaming of utopias. Rather, we are all designers with our feet firmly planted in the messiness of this world we call home, the world where children play, the world where we breathe the same air as elephants, sparrows, and Wilson's mites. Can we design for this world in a way that allows the future to be better?

Have we gone far enough? Can we take a few more steps?

Such a conception of designing is not easy. Rather, designing is like being in love. It pierces at the core of what it is to be human and mocks binaries such as logic and intuition. It can connect two people or twenty or two billion. It seems natural to extend designing to animals and plants, to any sentient being, even to beings from another planet. It feels universal, something everyone can understand and relate to, and yet every narration—like every story of boy meets girl, boy meets boy, girl meets girl, or human meets human—uncovers another layer, a detailing that makes it incapable of being captured in an equation. There is an elusiveness, an almost fugitive quality. Even after writing an entire book on it, it feels like we have translated a poem. Something remains ineffable.

We continue to ask ourselves, "Have we gone far enough? Can we take a few more steps?"

Appendix A: A Vocabulary for Designing

In this book, we introduce certain concepts and terms that for us constitute a vocabulary that lets us describe the dialogue in designing in all its richness. Below is a list of all those concepts and terms. The explanations provided below are not meant to be comprehensive; rather, they are indicative of key ideas.

1. Dialogue: The continuous temporal process that mediates and transforms the circular relationship between the parts and the whole.
2. Circular relationship: A relationship where you need to know the parts in order to know the whole and need to know the whole in order to know the parts.
3. Temporary closure: A halt in a dialogue. We halt, knowing that we can and will continue. A temporary closure is a whole (which could be a part). All parts and wholes are temporary closures. Everything we do is a temporary closure because at some point we stop and move on, and this includes our understanding of what temporary closure means.
4. Whole: A dialogue between the whole and the parts. It is a temporary closure.
5. Part: A portion of a whole. Wholes act as parts, too, and are in a dialogue with each other. A part is a temporary closure.
6. Complex system: A dialogue between a large number of diverse parts and wholes. It is a temporary closure.
7. Model: A representation of a particular configuration of a parts-whole relationship. It is a temporary closure. A dialogue is an act of continuous modeling.

8. Modeling: Creating a representation of a particular configuration of a parts-whole relationship. The dialogue in designing is a process of continuous modeling.

9. Design context: The place where designing takes place. It is a temporary closure and a dialogue between the problem space, the social space, and the institutional space.

10. Designing: A dialogue between context, designers, shared memory, and the artifact.

11. Artifact: The thing that is being designed. It is a temporary closure of the dialogue in designing.

12. Designers: People who design. They are part of a temporary closure. A dialogue takes place between context, designers, shared memory, and the artifact.

13. Shared memory: A living memory of the what, how, who, and why of designing. It is a temporary closure. It is a dialogue between designing, context, shared memory, and artifacts.

14. Conceptual flat space: The space that facilitates the dialogue in designing, where parts and wholes can be flattened and be composed together in different ways. It is a temporary closure.

15. Boundary objects and cognitive scaffolds: Models. They are temporary closures. They are the mediators of the dialogue in designing.

16. Theory of the artifact: A state of the artifact, a pause in the dialogue in designing articulated through models. It is a temporary closure.

17. Theory of designing: A theory of artifact, with designing as the artifact. It is a temporary closure.

The Story of Designing So Far

Figure A.1
Diverse people come together.

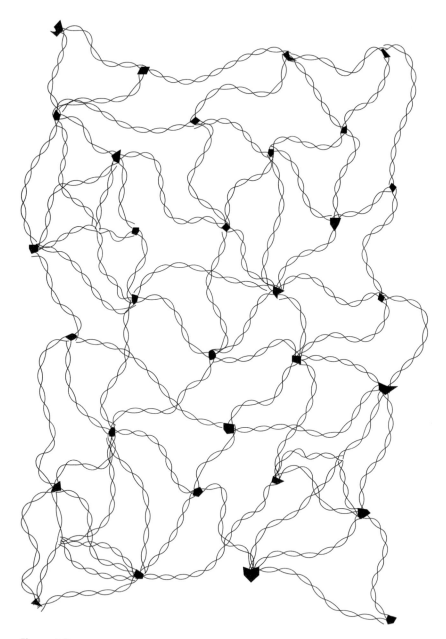

Figure A.2
They have a dialogue.

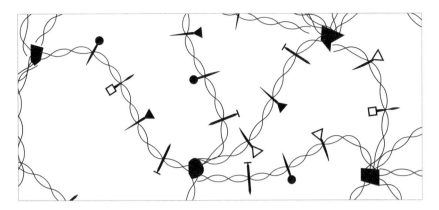

Figure A.3
The dialogue in designing is mediated by models, which includes boundary objects and cognitive scaffolds.

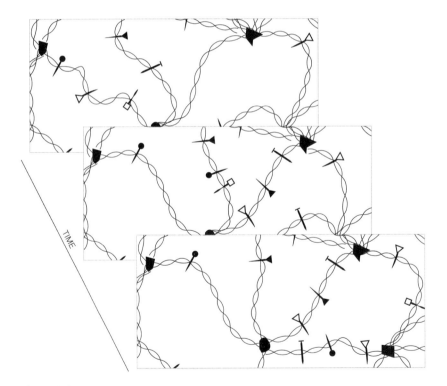

Figure A.4
The dialogue in designing can be seen as an act of continuous modeling. Temporary closures punctuate the dialogue. The state of the artifact keeps evolving during the dialogue. The theory of the artifact, which is a shared understanding of the state of the artifact, resides in the models, the artifact being designed, and the people involved in the dialogue.

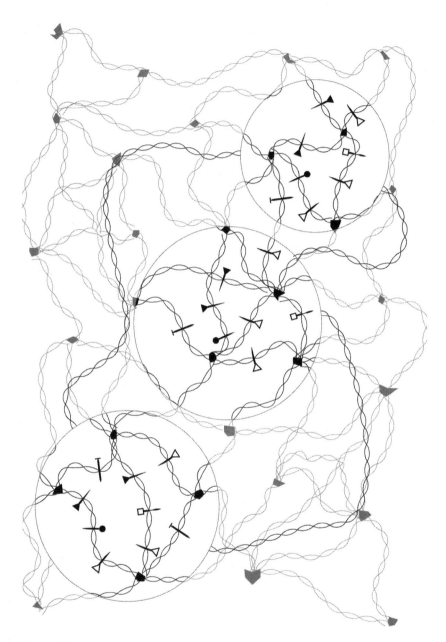

Figure A.5
The process of designing is a dialogue with other models, artifacts, and perspectives, which are all part of the shared memory—a living repository of the knowledge associated with designing.

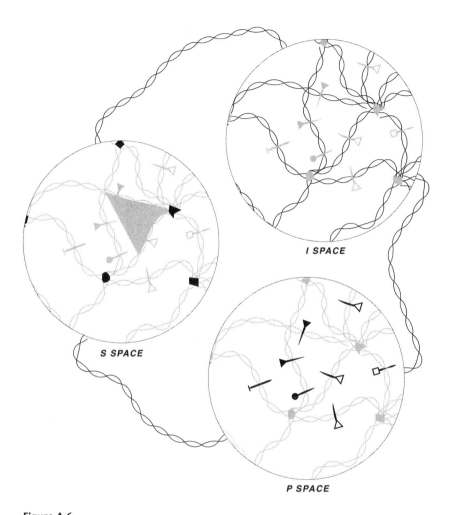

Figure A.6

The dialogue is a context-dependent process. We use the PSI (problem space, social space, institutional space) framework to characterize and provide insights into the context. The P space gives you insights on what is the problem being addressed, the S space gives you insights on who designs, and the I space gives you insights on the state of the dialogue or the how.

Appendix B: The Story of *n*-Dim

Our journey started a long time ago, and as these stories usually begin, it started with a challenge. In 1987, John Gallagher, then an adviser to the chief executive officer of Westinghouse and a nuclear engineer, asked us, a group of engineers, to study a design group that was creating new control systems for thermal plants before we designed the computational system that would support the group's design activity. During the course of this study and the next, our team of engineers and a computer scientist was augmented with two cognitive engineers and a nuclear engineer. Soon the group involved a chemical engineer, a philosopher, a sociologist, a pro-grammer/musician, and a public policy researcher. We worked with indus-try, too, which included managers, computer scientists, and engineers.

Our group mirrored the vision of design we conceptualized and created a computational support system. A multidisciplinary team of people with different cultural backgrounds and practical experiences molded, blended, and reconciled views and ideas over an extended time period. Over the next sixteen years (1987 to 2003), we performed detailed studies of the engi-neering practices of seven engineered products in four countries (Germany, Norway, Sweden, and the United States) and brief studies of four products in a single country (Japan). The product designs we studied included con-sumer products (such as power tools and consumer electronics) and heavy industrial products (such as hydroelectric turbines, switchgears, transform-ers, and trains).[1]

We designed a computational support system that could support our vision of designing as a multidisciplinary, complex, and dynamic process. We called it *n*-dim, which stood for *n*-dimensional information modeling. The primary activity *n*-dim supported was that of modeling, the way we described in this chapter. People could create different kinds of models, including text, graphics, movies, indices, and different classifications models (which in turn are models themselves). In short, n-dim supported any model that could be digitally stored. All models resided in a conceptual flat space. A model in the flat space could be inserted into new models, thus breaking the usual hierarchical way of constructing information. The same model could be given different names by different designers, thus allowing the designers to reuse models and refer to them using their own disciplinary language. Our n-dim modeling thus became a tool for supporting the dialogue between designers, between designers and themselves, and between disciplines.

Occasionally, a particular model that combined other models with interesting useful relationships among them would be recognized as having a useful structure. It was a modeling language from which other models with such structures could be constructed. This gave rise to different languages that were useful for different disciplines, such as languages for modeling processes or argumentations, product structures, or company procedures. New modeling languages enrich the ability to conduct an effective dialogue.

When different people collaborated together, they had a shared workspace where they could share models, comment, discuss, deliberate, and eventually agree on a consensual model. A traceable history was maintained, too, to ensure that you could track the development of the theory of the artifact. The corpus of shared models grew over time, which in turn contributed to the shared memory.

But our understanding of design as an evolving process with temporary closures but no perfection demanded that n-dim had to be designed in a nontraditional way. It had to be designed so it could constantly be changed as our understanding of design changed, as new technologies became available, and as new design challenges or contexts were attempted. Thus, n-dim model development was handled as another artifact.

Our n-dim was a complex product that required an understanding of the social sciences, engineering, programming, user interfaces, collaborative work, management, and many other disciplines that are necessary to understand and support a diverse group of people doing real design.

Such a collaboration between different disciplines was possible because our group operated as a nonhierarchical, open, and dialogical space. Working at CMU, with its interdisciplinary tradition, and with a group that was culturally and ideologically diverse and committed to the quest to understand designing in all its richness allowed us to push the boundaries of interdisciplinary research to question the nature of interdisciplinarity itself.

Although the original group has changed, the work continues with different people from other backgrounds joining us in this journey.

The *n*-Dim Community

The following people have been integral to the *n*-dim community in shaping the ideas from 1988 to the present, in chronological order of their appearance:

Eswaran Subrahmanian

Arthur Westerberg

Gregg Podnar

Sean N. Levy

Suresh L. Konda

Yoram Reich

Ira Monarch

Philip Sargent

Eric Gardner

Mark Thomas

Douglas Cunningham

Robert Patrick

Helen Granger

Joseph G. Davis

Jayachandra Reddy

Pranab K. Nag

Michael Collins

Christopher Lee

Bayani Caes

Katherine Prevost

Erica Fleckenstein

Tanya Rado

Anish Srivastava

Sebastiaan Meijer

Sruthi Krishnan

Over the years, the group has written many reports and papers that serve as our shared memory of the project. The following chronological list includes the reports of the studies done on design and engineering in Germany, Japan, Norway, Sweden, and the United States:

Subrahmanian, Eswaran, Susan Finger, and Tom Mitchell. "A Report on the NSF-EDRC Study of Product Design Processes in Selected Japanese Companies." EDRC Research Report 05-75-93, 1993.

Subrahmanian, Eswaran, and Ellen Daleng. "Information Flow Analysis of Hydro Power Design at Drummen." ABB R&D report. ABB Corporate Research, Norway, September 1993.

Subrahmanian, Eswaran. "Study of Reuse in Switchgear Design: An Information Flow Analysis-Based Study at ABB Distribution at Skein." ABB R&D report. ABB Corporate Research, Norway, June1995.

Subrahmanian, Eswaran, Andrea Jahnke, Harald Mackamul, and Thomas Schwab. "Information Flow Analysis of Product Development at Bosch Power Tools at Leinfelden." Robert Bosch R&D report. Robert Bosch Corporate R&D, Schillerhoe, June 1997.

Subrahmanian Eswaran, and Edgar Jellum. "Total Plant Engineering: An Information Flow Study of Total Power Plant Engineering at ABB." ABB R&D report. ABB Corporate Research, Norway, May 1998.

Subrahmanian, Eswaran, Helen Granger, and Russ Milliken. "A Report on the Study of the Design and Engineering Change Process at Adtranz." November 2000.

Subrahmanian, Eswaran, Christopher Lee, and Helen Granger. "Managing and Supporting Product Life Cycle through Engineering Change Management for a Complex Product." *Research in Engineering Design* 26, no. 3 (2015): 189–217.

Some additional papers by the group include the following:

Davis, J. G., E. Subrahmanian, S. Konda, H. Granger, M. Collins, and A. W. Westerberg. "Creating Shared Information Spaces to Support Collaborative Design Work." *Information Systems Frontiers* 3, no. 3 (2001): 377–392.

Konda, S., I. Monarch, P. Sargent, and E. Subrahmanian. "Shared Memory in Design: A Unifying Theme for Research and Practice." *Research in Engineering Design* 4, no. 1 (1992): 23–42.

Monarch, A. M., S. L. Konda, S. N. Levy, Y. Reich, E. Subrahmanian, and C. Ulrich. "Mapping Sociotechnical Networks in the Making." In *Social Science, Technical Systems, and Cooperative Work: Beyond the Great Divide*, edited by Geoffrey C. Bowker, Susan Leigh Star, William Turner, and Less Gasser, 331–354. Mahwah, NJ: Lawrence Erlbaum, 1997.

Reddy, J. M., S. Finger, S. Konda, and E. Subrahmanian. "Design as Building and Reusing Artifact Theories: Understanding and Supporting Growth of Design Knowledge." In *The Design Productivity Debate*, edited by Alex H. B. Duffy, 268–290. London: Springer, 1998.

Reich, Y., S. L. Konda, I. A. Monarch, S. N. Levy, and E. Subrahmanian. "Varieties and Issues of Participation and Design." *Design Studies* 17, no. 2 (1996): 165–180.

Reich, Y., S. L. Konda, E. Subrahmanian, D. Cunningham, A. Dutoit, R. Patrick, M. Thomas, and A. W. Westerberg. "Building Agility for Developing Agile Design Information Systems." *Research in Engineering Design* 11, no. 2 (1999): 67–83.

Sargent, P., E. Subrahmanian, M. Downs, R. Greene, and D. Rishel. "Materials' Information and Conceptual Data Modeling." In *Computerization and Networking of Materials Databases*, 3rd vol., edited by Thomas I. Barry and Keith W. Reynard, 1140, 172. Philadelphia: American Society for Testing and Materials, 1992.

Subrahmanian, E., R. Coyne, S. Konda, S. Levy, R. Martin, I. Monarch, Y. Reich, and A. Westerberg. "Support System for Different-Time Different-Place Collaboration for Concurrent Engineering." In *Proceedings of the Second IEEE Workshop on Enabling Technologies: Infrastructure for Collaborative Enterprises (WET-ICE)*, 187–191. Los Alamitos, CA: IEEE Computer Society Press, 1993.

Subrahmanian, E., S. L. Konda, S. N. Levy, Y. Reich, A.W. Westerberg, and I. Monarch. "Equations Aren't Enough: Informal Modeling in Design." *AI EDAM* 7, no. 4 (1993): 257–274.

Subrahmanian, E., and Y. Reich. "Advancing Problem Definition and Concept Generation for Improved Product Life Cycle." Paper presented at the International Conference on Trends in Product Life Cycle, Modeling, Simulation and Synthesis, PLMSS-2006, Bangalore, India, December 18–20, 2006.

Subrahmanian, E., Y. Reich, S. L. Konda, A. Dutoit, D. Cunningham, R. Patrick, M. Thomas, and A. W. Westerberg. "The *n*-Dim Approach to Creating Design Support Systems." In *Proceedings of ASME Design Theory and Methodology DTM '97*. Pittsburgh: American Society of Mechanical Engineers, 1997.

Subrahmanian, E., A. W. Westerberg, and G. Podnar. "Towards a Shared Information Environment for Engineering Design." In *Lecture Notes in Computer Science: Collaborative Product Development*, edited by D. Sriram, R. Logcher, and S. Fukuda, 200–226. Berlin: Springer-Verlag, 1991.

Notes

Chapter 1

1. The five elements are earth, water, fire, air, and space.

Chapter 2

1. One early version of this chapter was more than eighty pages long when we began the arduous process of editing it down to a more manageable length. Although there were many other designers and theorists whose contributions to designing we wished to keep—including Buckminster Fuller, Victor Papanek, and E. F. Schumacher—we had to eliminate them to keep the chapter length reasonable and ensure that the narrative of the shared memory of designing remained comprehensive.

The shared memory of designing presented in this chapter also does not include narratives from other geographies and contexts. For instance, we have begun researching the history of design in India to inform the narrative of Indian design as it stands now. We also hope to expand the scope of our inquiry to look into other such narratives because the strength of shared memory is found in enriching its diversity. As always, we consider this a temporary closure and not a full stop.

2. In his essay "Designing Ourselves," Daniel Miller writes: "What does it mean to suggest we are all museum curators? Well, to curate is to feel responsible for, and look after, the objects in your possession. To be a museum curator suggests that at least some of these objects will be chosen for public display, and these will illustrate some theme. … At some level, the sense that individuals have selected from their possessions which objects to display, and given thought to how they will be organized and presented, makes it reasonable to see a normal householder as at least analogous to a museum curator." Daniel Miller, "Designing Ourselves," in *Design Anthropology: Object Culture in the Twenty-first Century,* ed. Alison J. Clarke (New York: Springer, 2010), 88–99.

3. George Basalla, *The Evolution of Technology* (New York: Cambridge University Press, 1988), 8–10.

4. Basalla, *The Evolution of Technology*.

5. Vitruvius, *The Ten Books on Architecture*, trans. Morris Hickey Morgan (Cambridge, MA: Harvard University Press, 1914), *The Project Gutenberg*, 2006, http://www.guten berg.org/files/20239/20239-h/29239-h.htm.

6. Vitruvius, *The Ten Books*.

7. Robert John Goldwater and Marco Treves, eds., *Artists on Art: From the Fourteenth to the Twentieth Century* (New York: Pantheon, 1945), 45.

8. Yves Deforge, "Avatars of Design: Design before Design," in *The Idea of Design: A Design Issues Reader*, ed. Richard Buchanan and Victor Margolin, 21–28 (Cambridge, MA: MIT Press, 1995), 23.

9. A community of practice is a collection of people whose interactions with each other and communications on a regular basis are rooted in sharing a common inter-est or profession. The term was introduced by Jean Lave and Etienne Wenger as a means to develop a theory of social learning, and it has been used to understand the sociolinguistic basis on which members of a community learn from each other. The learning takes place as part of a joint activity or mutual engagement and is not nec-essarily based on belonging to a particular group or being in same place. It may even arise informally. Meetups in the social media world are an example. See Jean Lave and Etienne Wenger, *Situated Learning: Legitimate Peripheral Participation* (New York: Cambridge University Press, 1991); and Jean Lave and Etienne Wenger, *Communities of Practice: Learning, Meaning, and Identity* (Cambridge: Cambridge University Press, 1998).

10. Eugene S. Ferguson, *Engineering and the Mind's Eye* (Cambridge, MA: MIT Press, 1994).

11. Joel Mokyr, *The Gifts of Athena: Historical Origins of the Knowledge Economy* (Princeton, NJ: Princeton University Press, 2002).

12. Mokyr, *The Gifts of Athena*, 145.

13. Mokyr, *The Gifts of Athena*, 33.

14. Mokyr, *The Gifts of Athena*, 32.

15. Mokyr, *The Gifts of Athena*, 36–37.

16. Mokyr, *The Gifts of Athena*, 35.

17. In the essay "Rhetoric, Humanism, and Design," Richard Buchanan writes: "It is true that in the period from the Renaissance to the early days of the Industrial Revolution, the invention of techniques for mass production in support of the prac-tical arts allowed—and required—a separation of designing from making. However, design was also separated from intellectual and fine arts, leaving it without an intel-lectual foundation of its own." Richard Buchanan and Victor Margolin, eds., *Dis-covering Design: Explorations in Design Studies* (Chicago: University of Chicago Press, 1995), 34.

18. The first elucidation of the division of labor was postulated by Adam Smith in his pin factory example to illustrate the power of parallel production of parts and their combination to increase productivity. Subsequently, Charles Babbage provided the logic of the division of labor for the rising Industrial Revolution. Babbage, the

inventor of the calculating machine, showed through his own example of a pin factory that by separating the types of activities and skills and providing wages based on the demand for that particular class of labor, the new factory could reduce the cost of labor in contrast to having a single man do all of the work that constituted different types of skills. He also identified the fact that as workers learn their trades, they will improve their productivity over time

The work of Babbage goes beyond differential wages for differential skills to include the introduction of machinery in the factory. He advocated the use of a single source of power to combine parts of labor, replacing many people with a single person. In elaborating this argument, he also mentions technological innovations leading to the introduction of machinery and the continual improvements of machinery driving overall productivity. Further, Babbage envisioned a day when a calculating machine could replace an expensive mathematician for doing mundane calculative tasks in a factory.

A summary of Babbage's work narrated by Nathan Rosenberg also mentions that Babbage advocated the division of labor not just in the factory but also in the sciences as an important way that a society can maintain a competitive advantage in developing new technological innovations for improving its industry and competing in the global market. As can be seen in the evolution of industrialization, many of Babbage's ideas continue to prevail in the way that today's economies work. Babbage's pioneering economic analysis of an industrializing world influenced greatly the work of John Stuart Mill and Karl Marx in their analyses of industrializing societies. See Adam Smith, *The Wealth of Nations*, ed. Andrew S. Skinner, vol. 3 (New York: Prometheus Books, 1991); Nathan Rosenberg, "Charles Babbage: Pioneer Economist," in *Exploring the Black Box: Technology, Economics and History*, 24–46 (Cambridge: Cambridge University Press, 1994).

19. Bernhard E. Bürdek, *Design: History, Theory, and Practice of Product Design* (Basel: Birkhäuser Architecture, 2005), 19–23; Buchanan and Margolin, *Discovering Design*, 35.

20. Bürdek, *Design*, 23.

21. Bürdek, *Design*, 27.

22. Bürdek, *Design*, 27.

23. Bürdek, *Design*, 25.

24. Bürdek, *Design*, 28.

25. Walter Gropius, *Scope of Total Architecture* (London: G. Allen & Unwin, 1956), 19–20, as cited in Buchanan and Margolin, *Discovering Design*, 35–36.

26. The 1919 slogan "Art and Craft: A New Unity" is described in the four-page manifesto by Gropius, and at the opening of the Bauhaus exhibition in 1923, Gropius spoke about the new slogan "Art and Technology: A New Unity." For more details, see Bauhaus online, "Manifesto," http://bauhaus-online.de/en/atlas/das -bauhaus/idee/manifest (accessed July 6, 2016); Bauhaus online, "1923," http:// bauhaus-online.de/en/atlas/jahre/1923 (accessed July 6, 2016).

27. Bürdek, *Design*, 29.

28. Richard Buchanan, "Rhetoric, Humanism, and Design," in Buchanan and Margolin. *Discovering Design*, 38.

29. Alain Findeli, "Moholy-Nagy's Design Pedagogy in Chicago (1937–46)," in Buchanan and Margolin, *The Idea of Design*, 43.

30. Buchanan and Margolin, *The Idea of Design*, 43.

31. Buchanan and Margolin, *Discovering Design*, 39.

32. Buchanan and Margolin, *Discovering Design*, 41.

33. Bürdek, *Design*, 45.

34. Buchanan and Margolin, *Discovering Design*, 41.

35. Bürdek, *Design*, 51.

36. Nigan Bayazit, "Investigating Design: A Review of Forty Years of Design Research," *Design Issues* 20, no. 1 (2004): 18.

37. Bayazit, "Investigating Design," 18.

38. Bürdek, *Design*, 253.

39. The need and desirability of diversity has been argued for in different contexts; see Scott E. Page, *The Difference: How the Power of Diversity Creates Better Groups, Firms, Schools, and Societies* (Princeton, NJ: Princeton University Press, 2008). A concrete example of how diversity is used to bootstrap design and mathematics is presented in Yoram Reich, Offer Shai, Eswaran Subrahmanian, Armand Hatchuel, and Pascal Le Masson, "The Interplay between Design and Mathematics: Introduction to Bootstrapping Effects," in *Proceedings of the Ninth Biennial Conference on Engineering Systems Design and Analysis (ASME 2008)* (New York: American Society of Mechanical Engineers, 2008), 223–228.

40. Bayazit, "Investigating Design," 19.

41. Herbert A. Simon, *The Sciences of the Artificial* (Cambridge, MA: Massachusetts Institute of Technology, 1981), xi.

42. Simon, *The Sciences of the Artificial*, xi.

43. Simon, *The Sciences of the Artificial*, 129.

44. Simon, *The Sciences of the Artificial*, 129.

45. Simon, *The Sciences of the Artificial*, 130.

46. Simon, *The Sciences of the Artificial*, 130.

47. Newell, Allen, and Herbert A. Simon, *Human Problem Solving* (Englewood Cliffs, NJ: Prentice-Hall, 1972).

48. Herbert A. Simon, "From Substantive to Procedural Rationality," in *Twenty-five Years of Economic Theory: Retrospect and Prospect*, ed. T. J. Kastelein, S. K. Kuipers, W. A. Nijenhuis, and G. R. Wagenaar (Boston: Martinus Nijhoff Social Sciences Division, 1976), 65–86.

49. In explaining Herbert A. Simon's conception of the architecture of complexity, P. E. Agre argues that Simon's view of the architecture of complexity was shaped by the intellectual environment of his time by embodying the goals of general systems theory to create mathematical structures beyond a given context. Simon chose a tree structure as the basis for decomposition of all the systems that he saw around him. These included human organizational structures, the human body, the clock, and

others. In contrast, modern organizational structures include levels and networks to deal with complexity. P. E. Agre, "Hierarchy and History in Simon's 'Architecture of Complexity,'" *Journal of the Learning Sciences* 12, no. 3 (2003): 413–426.

50. Herbert A. Simon, "The Science of Design and the Architecture of Complexity," in Simon, *The Sciences of the Artificial*, 192–229.

51. Bayazit, "Investigating Design," 20–21.

52. Horst W. J. Rittel and Melvin M. Webber, "Dilemmas in a General Theory of Planning," *Policy Sciences* 4, no. 2 (1973): 155–169.

53. Bayazit, "Investigating Design," 20–21, citing Nigel Cross.

54. Werner Kunz and Horst W. J. Rittel, "Issues as Elements of Information Systems," Working Paper 131, Institute of Urban and Regional Development, University of California, Berkeley, 1970.

55. Christopher Alexander, *A Pattern Language: Towns, Buildings, Construction* (New York: Oxford University Press, 1977).

56. Bürdek, *Design*, 257.

57. Donald A. Schön, *The Reflective Practitioner: How Professionals Think in Action* (New York: Basic Books, 1983).

58. Schön, *The Reflective Practitioner*, 50.

59. Schön, *The Reflective Practitioner*, 21.

60. Schön, *The Reflective Practitioner*, 40.

61. Schön, *The Reflective Practitioner*, 50.

62. Gerhard Pahl, Wolfgang Beitz, Jörg Feldhusen, and Karl-Heinrich Grote, *Engineering Design: A Systematic Approach*, 3rd ed. (London: Springer, 2007).

63. Vladimir Hubka and W. Ernst Eder, "A Scientific Approach to Engineering Design," *Design Studies* 8, no. 3 (1987): 123–137; Vladimir Hubka and W. Ernst Eder, *Theory of Technical Systems: A Total Concept Theory for Engineering Design* (London: Springer, 1988); Vladimir Hubka and W. Ernst Eder, *Design Science: Introduction to the Needs, Scope, and Organization of Engineering Design Knowledge* (London: Springer, 1996).

64. Hiroyuki Yoshikawa, "General Design Theory and a CAD System," in *Man-Machine Communication in CAD/CAM, Proceedings of the IFIP WG5.2–5.3 Working Conference 1980 (Tokyo)*, ed. Toshio Sata and Ernest Warman, 35–57 (Amsterdam: North-Holland, 1981).

65. T. Tomiyama and H. Yoshikawa, "Extended General Design Theory," Technical Report CS-R8604, Centre for Mathematics and Computer Science, Amsterdam, 1986; Yoram Reich, "A Critical Review of General Design Theory," *Research in Engineering Design* 7, no. 1 (1995): 1–18.

66. Bill Hillier, John Musgrave, and Pat O'Sullivan, "Knowledge and Design," in *Environmental Design: Research and Practice*, ed. William J. Mitchell, 29.3.1–29.3.14 (Los Angeles: University of California, 1972).

67. Nigel Cross, *Engineering Design Methods* (Chichester: Wiley, 1989).

68. Armand Hatchuel and Benoit Weil, "CK Design Theory: An Advanced Formulation," *Research in Engineering Design* 19, no. 4 (2009): 181–192; Armand Hatchuel

and Benoit Weil, "A New Approach of Innovative Design: An Introduction to CK Theory," in *Proceedings of ICED 03, the Fourteenth International Conference on Engineering Design* (Stockholm: Design Society, 2003).

69. Louis L. Bucciarelli, *Engineering Philosophy* (Delft: Dup Satellite, 2003), 9; see also Louis L. Bucciarelli, *Designing Engineers* (Cambridge, MA: MIT Press, 1994).

70. Buchanan, "Rhetoric, Humanism, and Design," in Buchanan and Margolin, *Discovering Design*, 46.

71. Buchanan, "Rhetoric, Humanism, and Design."

72. Eugene S. Ferguson, in his book *Engineering: The Mind's Eye*, explores historical use of sketches and diagrams as an important medium of communication. He mentions the use of linear perspective, an isometric view, and the exploded diagrams created during the Renaissance as more precise models in drawings that facilitated better communications with fabricators and maintainers of the artifact. The work of Willemien Visser, of Julie Hesier, Barbara Tversky, and Mia Silverman, and of Masaki Suwa and BarbaraTversky in their studies of sketches from a cognitive perspective identify their use in translating concepts, negotiating, and arriving at a consensus in describing the various aspects of the artifact, especially in collaborative designing. Beyond verbal languages, sketches form an important part of the medium of designing, including the use of precise notational visual languages, such as an engineering drawing. See Ferguson, *Engineering and the Mind's Eye*; Willemien Visser, "Designing as Construction of Representations: A Dynamic Viewpoint in Cognitive Design Research," *Human–Computer Interaction* 21, no. 1 (2006): 103–152; Julie Heiser, Barbara Tversky, and Mia Silverman, "Sketches for and from Collaboration," *Visual and Spatial Reasoning in Design III*, ed. John S. Gero, Barbara Tversky, and Terry Knight, 69–78 (Sydney: Key Centre of Design Computing and Cognition, University of Sydney, 2004); Masaki Suwa and Barbara Tversky, "What Do Architects and Students Perceive in Their Design Sketches? A Protocol Analysis," *Design Studies* 18, no. 4 (1997): 385–403.

Chapter 3

1. Italo Calvino, *Mr. Palomar* (1983), trans. William Weaver (London: Vintage, 1999).

2. Calvino, *Mr. Palomar*, 3–4.

3. Calvino, *Mr. Palomar*, 5.

4. Edgar Morin, "Restricted Complexity, General Complexity," in *Worldviews, Science and Us: Philosophy and Complexity*, ed. Carlos Gershenson, Diederik Aerts, and Bruce Edmonds, 5–29 (Singapore: World Scientific Publishing, 2007), 6.

5. Richard Nisbett, *The Geography of Thought: How Asians and Westerners Think Differently ... and Why* (New York: Simon and Schuster, 2004), 20.

6. Juval Portugali brings in cognition of agents who live in the city to explore a perspective where he elaborates how the city and its citizens mutually influence

each other. By combining hard and soft sciences, he provides a means to understand the controlled emergence of a complex system consisting of interacting agents—a city. Juval Portugali, *Complexity, Cognition and the City* (New York: Springer Science & Business Media, 2011).

7. Pankaj Ghemawat with Steve Singer, "Redefining Global Strategy," podcast, *Harvard Business Review*, https://hbr.org/2007/09/harvard-business-ideacast-59-r.html (accessed December 28, 2018; see also Pankaj Ghemawat, *Redefining Global Strategy: Crossing Borders in a World Where Differences Still Matter* (Cambridge, MA: Harvard University Press, 2007).

8. Palagummi Sainath, *Everybody Loves a Good Drought: Stories from India's Poorest Districts* (Delhi: Penguin Books India, 1996), 5–9.

9. Although most sophisticated analysts understand that physical investment alone will not automatically lead to development, government and other organizations create plan after plan without taking this lesson into account. William Easterly recounts different examples of such nonholistic development solutions of the World Bank that failed. William Easterly, *The Elusive Quest for Growth: Economists' Adventures and Misadventures in the Tropics* (Cambridge, MA: MIT Press, 2001). The narrowness of dominant approaches to development is documented in William Easterly, *Tyranny of Experts* (New York: Basic Books, 2014), and in Courtney Keene, "Development Projects That Did Not Work: The Perils of Narrow Approaches to Complex Problems," Globalhood research report, October 2007, http://newmajoritylabs .com/wp-content/uploads/2015/11/Development_Projects_That_Didnt_Work.pdf (accessed August 26, 2015).

10. George Lakoff, *Don't Think of an Elephant! Know Your Values and Frame the Debate: The Essential Guide for Progressives* (White River Junction, VT: Chelsea Green, 2004).

11. Lakoff, *Don't Think of an Elephant*.

12. Jagdish Sharan Verma, Leila Seth, and Gopal Subramanian, "Report of the Committee on Amendments to Criminal Law, 2013," PRS Legislative Research, New Delhi, 2013.

13. Morin, "Restricted Complexity, General Complexity," 5.

14. Melanie Mitchell writes toward the conclusion of her book *Complexity: A Guided Tour*: "What should we call it? It is probably clear by now that this is the crux of the problem—we don't have the right vocabulary to precisely describe what we are studying. We use the words *complexity, self-organization*, and *emergence* to represent phenomena common to the systems we're interested, but we can't yet characterize the commonalties in a more rigorous way. We need a new vocabulary that not only captures the conceptual building blocks of self-organization and emergence but that can also describe how these come to encompass what we call *functionality, purpose,* or *meaning* (cf. chapter 12)." Melanie Mitchell, *Complexity: A Guided Tour* (New York: Oxford University Press, 2009), location 5016 of 7309 in Kindle ebook.

15. Morin, "Restricted Complexity, General Complexity," 8.

16. The human microbiome is an ecosystem of bacteria and their genetic elements residing in a human being. There are about 10 to 100 trillion bacteria in the gut

system of a human. Dwayne C. Savage, "Microbial Ecology of the Gastrointestinal Tract," *Annual Reviews in Microbiology* 31, no. 1 (1977): 107–133. These bacteria carry genetic information that far exceeds that of a human genome and is responsible to many life-dependent functions. National Institutes of Health, "NIH Human Microbiome Project Defines Normal Bacterial Makeup of the Body," news release, June 13, 2012, http://www.nih.gov/news/health/jun2012/nhgri-13.htm (accessed July 26, 2015). These bacteria also communicate among themselves by chemical signaling. Stephan Schauder and Bonnie L. Bassler, "The Languages of Bacteria," *Genes & Development* 15, no. 12 (2001): 1468–1480; see also Frizhoff Capra, *Web of Life: A New Scientific Understanding of Living Systems* (New York: Anchor, 1997).

17. Nisbett, *The Geography of Thought*, 52.

18. In his book on *Identity and Violence: Illusion of Destiny*, Amartya Sen identifies himself as an economist, a Bengali, an Indian, a professor, a feminist, a man, a believer in secular democracy, and so on—illustrating the multiple identities we all carry. When one identity dominates others, violence becomes an instrument. He claims that recognizing these multiple identities and having an ability to choose them to create a composite identity are antidotes to single dimensional identity that leads to violence. Amartya Sen, *Identity and Violence: The Illusion of Destiny* (Delhi: Penguin Books India, 2007).

19. In the *Mythical Man-Month*, Fred Brooks speaks about how adding more people to a software project does not necessarily mean it will go faster. The sum of more could be less than the sum of less. Frederick P. Brooks, *The Mythical Man-Month: Essays on Software Engineering*, 2nd ed. (Reading, MA: Addison-Wesley, 1995.

20. J. Christopher Jones, "How My Thoughts about Design Methods Have Changed during the Years," *Design Methods and Theories* 11, no. 1 (1977): 48–62.

21. John Ziman, "Is Science Losing Its Objectivity?," *Nature* 382, no. 6594 (1996): 751–754, 753; see also, John Ziman, "Emerging out of Nature into History: The Plurality of the Sciences," *Philosophical Transactions of the Royal Society of London A: Mathematical, Physical and Engineering Sciences* 361, no. 1809 (2003): 1617–1633.

22. Howard Gardner, *Five Minds for the Future* (Boston: Harvard Business Press, 2006).

23. Gardner, *Five Minds for the Future*.

24. Yoram Reich, Suresh L Konda., Ira A. Monarch, Sean N. Levy, and Eswaran Subrahmanian, "Varieties and Issues of Participation and Design," *Design Studies* 17, no. 2 (1996): 165–180.

Chapter 4

1. Brian Seibert, "Stillness and Motion and Voluptuous Curves, in a Temple Setting," dance review, *New York Times*, January 12, 2015, http://www.nytimes.com/2015/01/13/arts/dance/nrityagram-dancers-at-the-temple-of-dendur-at-the-met.html?_r=0.

2. Surupa Sen was interviewed by Sruthi Krishnan in July 2012.

3. The individual-centric model of cognition in design has dominated the study of designing for the last thirty years and still does implicitly in numerous studies in architecture, industrial design, automated designing, and computational support for designing. Challenges to the individual view of cognition have been to bring in context in different ways. The alternative conceptualization came from other cognitive scientists who found the purely computational individual centric model of cognition wanting. The computational symbolic system was challenged from different perspectives, including the embodiment of intelligence in the physical being, leading to calls for research into the relationships between the embodied and the external symbolic views of intelligence. F. Varela, E. Thompson, and E. Rosch, *The Embodied Mind: Cognitive Science and Human Experience* (Cambridge, MA: MIT Press, 1991); see also Andy Clark, *Being There: Putting Brain, Body, and World Together Again* (Cambridge, MA: MIT Press, 1998).

4. Situated cognition accepts the idea that a designer is working in a larger social context. In this model, the knowing and doing are interconnected. The knowledge is *situated* in the environmental and the sociocultural contexts. Lucy A. Suchman, *Plans and Situated Actions: The Problem of Human-Machine Communication* (Cambridge: Cambridge University Press, 1987). Cognition inherently has a dynamic character in its functioning where the knowledge of the situation mobilizes both situational and prior knowledge of the context of operation. A major impact of this perspective has been its use in designing joint planning of operations of human-robot cooperative system for the Mars rover. William J. Clancey, *Working on Mars: Voyages of Scientific Discovery with the Mars Exploration Rovers* (Cambridge, MA: MIT Press, 2012).

Situated cognition is directed at the origin and social maintenance of knowledge. The work on situated cognition in communities of practice of Jean Lave and Etienne Wenger is directed at the collective cognition of the practitioners and their tools and languages. The focus of this effort is to bring together the interactions between social and individual cognition. From this perspective, knowledge and semantics can arise out of an individual situated in the social, negotiated at the social, and providing the acceptance and institutionalization (inclusion in the community of practice) that, in turn, is interpreted in the individual. Jean Lave and Etienne Wenger, *Communities of Practice: Learning, Meaning, and Identity* (New York: Cambridge University Press, 1998).

5. E. Hutchins, "Distributed Cognition," in *International Encyclopedia of the Social and Behavioral Sciences*, ed. Neil J. Sonelser and Paul B. Baltes, 2068–2072 (Oxford: Elsevier Science, 2001).

6. Distributed cognition is focused on understanding the role of cognition in naturally occurring situated collective tasks. Originated by Edwin Hutchins with his study of navigation of the sea in the night by the indigenous people of Polynesia, it illustrates the use of the night sky and the environment as collective distributed external cognitive elements to decide the direction to proceed. Edwin Hutchins, *Cognition in the Wild* (Cambridge, MA: MIT Press, 1995).

In engineering design, J. S. Busby illustrated that a breakdown in distributed cognition of mediating representations can be the cause of failures. J. S. Busby, "Error and Distributed Cognition in Design," *Design Studies* 22, no. 3 (2001): 233–254.

The distributed cognition model has been used in a number of areas, including the study of cultural influences in use of coordinating artifacts (as in the case of the aircraft cockpit) to understand variations in behavior across cultures in their use. Edwin Hutchins, "How a Cockpit Remembers Its Speeds," *Cognitive Science* 19, no. 3 (1995): 265–288. Ronald Giere in his analysis of representations and models in science makes the case that these models and theories live in the distributed cognitive world of the scientists. Ronald Giere, "Scientific Cognition as Distributed Cognition," *The Cognitive Basis of Science*, ed. P. Carruthers, S. Stich, and M. Siegal, 285–299 (New York: Cambridge University Press, 2002).

7. Susan Leigh Star and James R. Griesemer, "Institutional Ecology, 'Translations' and Boundary Objects: Amateurs and Professionals in Berkeley's Museum of Vertebrate Zoology, 1907–39," *Social Studies of Science* 19 (3): 387–420.

8. Star and Griesemer, "Institutional Ecology." These words are from Annie Alexander.

9. Star and Griesemer, "Institutional Ecology."

10. Star and Griesemer, "Institutional Ecology."

11. The case of the mechanical engineer in a power equipment firm is a minimally fictionalized account of a real case study. For more details, refer to Susan Finger, Eswaran Subrahmanian, and Eric Gardner, "A Design System for Concurrent Engineering of Transformers," in *Proceedings of ICED 93 / Ninth International Conference on Engineering Design*, August 17–19, 1993, The Hague (Zurich: Heurista, 1993).

12. Suresh K. Bhavnani and Bonnie E. John, "The Strategic Use of Complex Computer Systems," *Human-Computer Interaction* 15, no. 2 (2000): 107–137.

13. Ulrich Flemming, Suresh K. Bhavnani, and Bonnie E. John, "Mismatched Metaphor: User vs System Model in Computer-Aided Drafting," *Design Studies* 18, no. 4 (1997): 349–368; Kathryn Henderson, *On Line and on Paper: Visual Representations, Visual Culture, and Computer Graphics in Design Engineering* (Cambridge, MA: MIT Press, 1999).

14. Finger, Subrahmanian, and Gardner, "A Design System."

15. Henry Petroski has explored the unifying theme of failures as a driver of design and invention and as an integral part of the shared memory of designing, through his numerous books. See Henry Petroski, *Design Paradigms: Case Histories of Error and Judgment in Engineering* (Cambridge: Cambridge University Press, 1994); and *Success through Failure: The Paradox of Design* (Princeton, NJ: Princeton University Press, 2006).

16. Throughout his career, the manager of the group doing process M had spent time in all aspects of engineering—design, R&D, manufacturing, and field installation—which led to his institution of procedures and a culture that created a minimal failure of organizational systems and products. Finger, Subrahmanian, and Gardner, "A Design System for Concurrent Engineering of Transformers."

17. Geoffrey C. Bowker and Susan Leigh Star call them boundary infrastructure. Through this distinction, they try to make a difference between objects that are the focus in the context of work and the infrastructure objects that serve as a boundary within a discipline or even subdiscipline. Geoffrey C. Bowker and Susan Leigh Star, *Sorting Things Out: Classification and Its Consequences* (Cambridge, MA: MIT Press, 2000).

18. Our view of designing where both the individual and the social are in a dialogue with each other is also bolstered by ethnographic studies of engineering design. Louis L. Bucciarelli, "An Ethnographic Perspective on Engineering Design," *Design Studies* 9, no. 3 (1988): 159–168.

Ethnographic studies of engineering design work, in groups and across disciplines, have taken the position that all engineering work is social and the processes are necessarily social. These studies, in contrast with traditional views of engineering as a pure problem-solving activity, provide an alternative view of designing as a social construction process that frames the problem and reconciles conflicting goals, objectives, tests, and the interpretations in the development of the product by participants. Linden J. Ball and Thomas C. Ormerod, "Putting Ethnography to Work: The Case for a Cognitive Ethnography of Design," *International Journal of Human-Computer Studies* 53, no. 1 (2000): 147–168. Bucciarelli, in reporting the main finding of his ethnographic study of design, claims that "different participants think about the work on design in quite different ways. They do not share fully congruent internal representations of the design. In this sense design at any time in the design process is more than the sum, or simple synthesis, of its participants' interpretation. In this sense it is a social construction." Bucciarelli, "An Ethnographic Perspective on Engineering Design," 166.

For the implementation of these ideas into the design support system *n*-dim see Yoram Reich, Suresh L. Konda, Eswaran Subrahmanian, Douglas Cunningham, Allen Dutoit, Robert Patrick, Mark Thomas, and Arthur W. Westerberg, "Building Agility for Developing Agile Design Information Systems," *Research in Engineering Design* 11, no. 2 (1999): 67–83; Eswaran Subrahmanian, Suresh L. Konda, Sean L. Levy, Yoram Reich, Arthur W. Westerberg, and Ira Monarch, "Equations Aren't Enough: Informal Modelling in Design," *AI EDAM* 7, no. 4 (1993): 257–274; Eswaran Subrahmanian, Yoram Reich, Suresh L. Konda, Allen Dutoit, Douglas Cunningham, Robert Patrick, Mark Thomas, and Arthur W. Westerberg. "The *n*-Dim Approach to Creating Design Support Systems," in *Proceedings of the 1997 ASME Design Engineering Technical Conferences: DETC '97* (New York: American Society of Mechanical Engineers, 1997); and E. Subrahmanian, A. W. Westerberg, and G. Podnar. "Towards Shared Information Models in Engineering Design," in *Lecture Notes in Collaborative Product Development*, ed. Duvvuru Sriram (London: Springer, 1991).

19. Writing about how the dialogue with Nrityagram infused a new energy into Kandyan, Sri Lankan writer Subha Wijesiriwardena says the following: "Let's recognize *Samhara* as a true turning point for the Chitrasena Dance Company, and therefore dance in Sri Lanka. It represents a kind of brand-new return to form, a restoration

and a revival of traditions and values close to Chitrasena's heart. One is of taking Sri Lankan dance to the world, and *Samhara* has reinstated the Chitrasena Company's place in the international dance world through its phenomenally successful tour. Another is presenting traditional dance as radical contemporary dance work, which *Samhara* has done successfully with Sen's choreography and the immense skill of all five dancers. The last is the important tradition of artistic collaboration. Much of Chitrasena's best work was created in close collaboration with musicians and artists who shared his values and artistic integrity. With *Samhara*, the Chitrasena Company returns to this idea, showing that perhaps their best work is created in partnership and friendship." Subha Wijesiriwardena, "What *Samhara* Means: A Review of *Samhara* and an Unraveling of What It Really Means for Sri Lankan Dance," blog, May 16, 2012, https://blogsmw.wordpress.com/2012/05/16/what-samhara-means-a-review-of-samhara-and-an-unraveling-of-what-it-really-means-for-sri-lankan-dance (accessed July 5, 2016).

20. Herbert H. Clark sees language as something similar, a joint activity. Instead of seeing language as an individual act that is situated within the domain of cognitive sciences such as cognitive psychology, linguistics, and philosophy or as a social act as described by social sciences, Clark contends that it belongs to both. Herbert H. Clark, *Using Language* (Cambridge: Cambridge University Press, 1996). This is in step with our conception of designing—an activity performed by individuals together, a participatory activity, a joint activity. And we take this one step further. An individual designing in our view is a form of collaboration with oneself and thus can be seen as a joint action, too. What is required for a joint activity to take place? Here Clark introduces the notion of a common ground: "Two people's common ground is, in effect, the sum of their mutual, common, or joint knowledge, beliefs, and suppositions." (The technical notion of a common ground was introduced by Robert Stalnaker. Refer to page 93 of Clark's *Using Language* for more details on the common ground.)

21. In line with Herbert H. Clark's study of the use of language, the work of Michael Tomasello focuses on a research program that aims at discovering patterns of use of language across primates and humans. Clark, *Using Language*; Michael Tomasello, *The Cultural Origins of Human Cognition* (Cambridge, MA: Harvard University Press, 2009). The distinctive feature of humans to use and evolve new languages is postulated to be a collection of constructs and the focus on the communicative aspects of the language. The cognitive linguistic account of language generation, variation, evolution, and use presented by Nick Chater and Morten H. Christiansen is in line with Tomasello's and Clark's use of language. Nick Chater and Morten H. Christiansen, "Language Acquisition Meets Language Evolution," *Cognitive Science* 34, no. 7 (2010): 1131–1157. Chater and Christiansen postulate that there are cognitive modules in the brain that allow for the composition of syntactic and semantic structures that are geared toward the ease of learning a language in a community.

22. Without cooperative aspects in the social context of human acts (such as designing), societies could not maintain a collective memory of its practices and the

ability to transfer it across generations. Further, this account of generations and use of language describes well the engineering approach to language. It needs to create useful structures that can be put together to create the meaning of the artifact from multiple perspectives (Monarch et al., 1997). Viewing designs as a social, cognitive, and linguistic process accords well with the cognitive-functional perspective of language. We contend that the evolution of formal languages, standards, and models accepted in community of practices follows a similar social, cognitive, functional, linguistic path in engineering practice.

Based on the studies quoted, we posit the characterization of language as a dynamic evolving functional artifact without a universal theory but with universal constructs. The same can be said of design where all different forms of representations—linguistic, nonlinguistic, and nonnotational—act together as collections of models and theories. They record, inform, create new knowledge, influence, and constrain how the designing progresses. They are part of the dialogue among ourselves and the world we inhabit in creating the artifacts around us. Understanding how these models are created, managed, shared, and understood is key to understanding the process of designing. See Suresh Konda, Ira Monarch, Philip Sargent, and Eswaran Subrahmanian, "Shared Memory in Design: A Unifying Theme for Research and Practice," *Research in Engineering Design* 4 no. 1 (1992): 23–42; Ira Monarch, Suresh L. Konda, Sean N. Levy, Yoram Reich, Eswaran Subrahmanian, and Carol Ulrich, "Mapping Sociotechnical Networks in the Making," in *Social Science, Technical Systems, and Cooperative Work: Beyond the Great Divide*, ed. Geoffrey C. Bowker, Susan Leigh Star, William Turner, and Les Gasser (Mahwah, NJ: Erlbaum, 1997), 331–354.

Chapter 5

1. James Bohman, "Critical Theory," *The Stanford Encyclopedia of Philosophy*, fall 2016 ed., ed. Edward N. Zalta, March 8, 2005, https://plato.stanford.edu/entries/critical-theory (accessed December 28, 2018).

2. The case study of Rubbish! is based on the second edition of the Design across Cultures project, a collaboration between Fields of View, Bangalore, and MediaLAB, Amsterdam. For more details on the project, please refer to Fields of View, "Rubbish!," Bangalore, India, 2017, http://fieldsofview.in/projects/rubbish. Sruthi Krishnan was part of the project.

3. Meera Srinivasan. "When a Trash Mountain Spelt Tragedy," *The Hindu*, April 22, 2017, https://www.thehindu.com/todays-paper/tp-international/when-a-trash-mountain-spelt-tragedy/article18193670.ece (accessed December 28, 2018).

4. Agence France-Presse in Addis Ababa, "Death Toll from Rubbish Dump Landslide in Ethiopia Rises to Sixty-five," *The Guardian*, March 13, 2017, https://www.theguardian.com/world/2017/mar/13/death-toll-rises-to-65-after-rubbish-dump-landslide-in-ethiopia (accessed December 28, 2018).

5. Sruthi Krishnan, "Scaling the Mountainous Problem of Garbage," *The Hindu*, May 4, 2017, accessed December 28, 2018, https://www.thehindu.com/thread/politics -and-policy/when-mountains-of-garbage-come-crashing-down/article18383260.ece (accessed December 28, 2018).

6. The work on cognitive functioning of models provides the basis for the study of model-based reasoning. It does not address how learning takes place through the use of models. Roland Frigg and Steven Hartmann use Hughes's DDI framework to explain learning from these models where the first D represents denotation of the target system, the second D represents demonstration to investigate theoretical claims, and I represents the interpretation of results. Frigg Roland and Steven Hartmann, "Scientific Models," in *The Philosophy of Science: An Encyclopedia*, vol. 2, ed. Sahotra Sarkar and Jessica Pfeifer (New York: Routledge, 2005).

Learning takes place through the use of experiments and simulations because there are no fixed rules for modeling. Matching the models to the target system takes place through the construction and manipulation of models, and it is through this process that an appropriate model is chosen. Physical models (such as scaled models of products) do not pose the same issues in the use of symbolic and other information-based models of the target system. Mathematical models can be subject to analytical methods for verification. On the other hand, simulation models are often used to deal with dynamics of time, and sometimes results from them could be potentially misleading. After the models are constructed, we need to map the results to the observables in the target system to understand the interpretation of the model. Given the variety of models, there are no specific methods to map them to the target system. In engineering, we often need overlaps from multiple models of the same phenomena to create a realistic mapping to the target systems. Zachary Pirtle, "How the Models of Engineering Tell the Truth," *Philosophy of Engineering and Technology*, vol. 2, ed. Pieter E. Vermaas, C. Didier, D. Cressman, N. Doorn, and B. Newberry (Basel: Springer Science + Business Media, 2010). Investigations into such questions are still open in the philosophical studies of construction, manipulation, and mapping of models to target systems in science and engineering.

7. Recent work in philosophy and practice of science has shifted the attention from studying the role of theories in science to the role of models in all sciences. See Mary S. Morgan and Margaret Morrison, *Models as Mediators: Perspectives on Natural and Social Science* (Cambridge: Cambridge University Press, 1999); their work on models as mediators takes the approach that models not only serve as mediators but also are autonomous in their existence and evolution. According to them, models play an autonomous role of mediators and dialogical devices between the scientific enquiry and nature. See also Lorenzo Magnani and Nancy J. Nersessian, *Model-Based Reasoning: Science, Technology, Values* (London: Springer, 2002); and Ronald N. Giere, "Using Models to Represent Reality," in *Model-Based Reasoning in Scientific Discovery*, ed. Lorenzo Magnani, Nancy J. Nersessian, and Paul Thagard (New York: Kluwer/ Plenum, 1999), 41–57.

Roman Frigg and Stephan Hartmann identify two different kinds of models used in science: models of phenomena and models of data. They play different roles. Models of phenomena represent a target system and assigning what it determines becomes an important question. Further, there are often multiple models of the same phenomenon that have different forms. For example, a computational fluid dynamics model of the wing of an aircraft is represented symbolically and is different from the scaled physical model of the wing; these models serve different purposes. See Roman Frigg and Stephan Hartmann, "Models in Science," in *The Philosophy of Science*, ed. S. Sarkar and J. Pfeifer (New York: Routledge, 2005), 740–749. In "Using Models," Giere points out that the representation of a model is based on the question being asked of the model by the investigator. In line with this notion, Frigg and Hartmann, in "Models in Science," present an ontology of scientific models. They include iconic models such as mice in clinical investigations in medicine, idealized models that abstract many aspects of the phenomenon such as use of point masses in Newton's gravitational theory, analogical models that are based on sharing a set of relationships such as model of the brain as a machine and, phenomenological models that are based on observables. Models of data do not assume a theory behind the data but derive a theory by eliminating errors from the observations and fit curves on the cleaned data. The work on the distinction between these models is a subject of inquiry in philosophy of science.

8. The discussion of the theory-practice debate manifests itself in different forms around us. The received view of theory-practice divide is best described by the French saying: "Theory is the general and practice is the soldier"; see W. Addis, *Structural Engineering: The Nature of Theory and Design* (Hemels, UK: Ellis Horwood, 1990). Addis rejects this view based on the history and evolution of structural engineering. Nevertheless, the basic-applied (theory-practice) divide attributed to Vannevar Bush's 1945 article, "Science: The Endless Frontier," is still predominant in the science policy world. See Vannevar Bush, Science: The Endless Frontier," *Transactions of the Kansas Academy of Science* 48, no. 3 (1945): 231–264.

Ben Shneiderman challenges the frame of basic-applied dichotomy to explore the bidirectional interdependence of basic and applied research through a number of case studies; see Ben Shneiderman, *The New ABCs of Research: Achieving Breakthrough Collaborations* (Oxford: Oxford University Press, 2016). The dominance and fallacy of Bush's view has also been critiqued by Venkatesh Naraynamurti, Tolu Odumosu, and Lee Vinsel by changing the frame from the basic-applied dichotomy to discovery-invention interdependence. They present an analysis of six Nobel prizes in physics and how the work of the winners reflect the interconnectedness of discoveries of phenomena and invention of artifacts. The above authors demonstrate through examples the importance of recognizing the bi-directional relationship between theory (basic) and practice (applied research) in the conception of science policy. See Venkatesh Narayanamurti, Tolu Odumosu, and Lee Vinsel, "RIP: The Basic/Applied Research Dichotomy," *Issues in Science and Technology* 29, no. 2 (2013): 31–36.

In the realm of engineering and technology Suresh Konda et al.'s conception of "shared memory" and Yoram Reich's exploration of "transcending the theory-practice problem of technology" argue for mutual bootstrapping in the context of design theories and design practice. See Suresh Konda, Ira Monarch, Philip Sargent, and Eswaran Subrahmanian, "Shared Memory in Design: A Unifying Theme for Research and Practice," *Research in Engineering Design* 4 no. 1 (1992): 23–42; and Yoram Reich, "Transcending the Theory-Practice Problem of Technology," EDRC Report 12-51-92, Engineering Design Research Center, Carnegie Mellon University, Pittsburgh, 1992.

Our position is that the collective knowledge embodied and generated through the bidirectional relationship between theory and practice is not separable.

9. Environmental Support Group, "Bangalore's Toxic Legacy Intensifies: Status of Landfills, Waste Processing Sites and Dumping Grounds, and Working Conditions of Pourakarmikas," Bangalore, India, http://www.indiaenvironmentportal.org.in/files/file/bangalore-s-toxic-legacy-intensifies.pdf (accessed December 28, 2018).

10. Sumit Chakraberty, "From Waste Picker to Recycling Manager," Citiscope, April 14, 2014, http://archive.citiscope.org/story/2014/waste-picker-recycling-manager (accessed December 28, 2018).

11. Pinky Chandran, Nalini Shekar, Marwan Abubaker, and Akshay Yadav, "Informal Waste Workers Contribution Bangalore," Working paper, Jain University, Bangalore, India, August 1, 2016, http://hasirudala.in/wp-content/uploads/2016/08/1.-Full-Paper-Chandran-Informal-Waste-Workers-Contribution-in-Bangalore-1.pdf. (accessed December 28, 2018).

12. Our conception of the dialogue in designing as modeling is about diverse disciplinary perspectives constructing and reconstructing information about what is being designed together as well as in their own disciplinary spaces. Luciano Floridi's work on philosophy of information, which deals with the method of abstraction and the ways that the different levels of abstraction interact with each other, is resonant with our work. Luciano Floridi, *The Philosophy of Information* (Oxford: Oxford University Press, 2011). For example, a material can be modeled in two ways. You can build a finite element model of the material for bulk properties (such as stress and strain), and you can also build a model for the atomistic behavior of the material. And both these models, at different levels of abstraction, allow us to understand, construct, and reconstruct information about the system behavior (at that particular level of abstraction) at hand, which is how we see the act of modeling in designing too.

13. Pascal Le Masson, Armand Hatchuel, and Benoit Weil identify the two different teaching strategies adopted by Paul Klee and Johannes Itten. Itten's pedagogy was based on separating colors, forms, texture, material, and structure: in effect he was decomposing the objects to create the ingredients in the conceptual flatspace. Meanwhile, Klee emphasized the creation of an image of the whole to construct the parts in relationship to the whole step by step. The combination of these approaches allows for teaching students the means by which to achieve generativity,

a fundamental and unique property of design that is afforded by the conceptual flatspace in the n-dim environment. For more information see Pascal Le Masson, Armand Hatchuel, and Benoit Weil, "Design Theory at Bauhaus: Teaching 'Splitting' Knowledge," *Research in Engineering Design* 27, no. 2 (2016): 91–115; and Armand Hatchuel, Pascal Le Masson, Yoram Reich, and Eswaran Subrahmanian, "Design Theory: The Foundations of a New Paradigm for Science and Engineering," *Research in Engineering Design* 29, no. 1 (2018): 5–21.

14. Jayachandra M. Reddy, Susan Finger, Suresh Konda, and Eswaran Subrahmanian, "Design as Building and Reusing Artifact Theories: Understanding and Supporting Growth of Design Knowledge." In *The Design Productivity Debate*, ed. Alex H. B. Duffy (London: Springer, 1998), 268–290.

15. Fields of View, "White Paper Documenting the Process of Designing Rubbish!," http://fieldsofview.in/publications/visuals/WhitePaperConverstation2014 (accessed December 28, 2018).

Chapter 6

1. The PSI (problem space, social space, institutional space) framework captures our long-term understanding of the role of context in design. It also evolved in the last years through further refinements as presented in the following papers: Sebastian Meijer, Yoram Reich, and Eswaran Subrahmanian, "The Future of Gaming for Design of Complex Systems," in *Back to the Future of Gaming*, ed. Richard D. Duke and Willy C. Kriz, 154–167 (Bielefeld: W. Bertelsmann, 2014); Yoram Reich and Eswaran Subrahmanian, "Designing PSI: An Introduction to the PSI Framework," in *Proceedings of the Twentieth International Conference on Engineering Design (ICED 15)*, Milan, Italy (Glasgow: Design Society, 2015); Yoram Reich and Eswaran Subrahmanian, "The PSI Matrix: A Framework and a Theory of Design," in *Proceedings of the Twenty-first International Conference on Engineering Design (ICED 17)*, Vancouver, Canada, August 21–25 (Glasgow: Design Society, 2017); Eswaran Subrahmanian, Yoram Reich, Frido Smulders, and Sebastian A. Meijer, "Design as a Synthesis of Spaces: Using the P-S Framework," *Proceedings of IASDR2011, the Fourth World Conference in Design Research*, Delft, The Netherlands (International Association of Societies of Design Research, 2011); Eswaran Subrahmanian, Yoram Reich, Frido Smulders, and Sebastian A. Meijer, "Designing: Insights from Weaving Theories of Cognition and Design Theories," in *Proceedings of the Eighteenth International Conference on Engineering Design (ICED '11)*, Copenhagen, Denmark (Glasgow: Design Society, 2011).

Our research on designing and specifically on PSI continues to evolve as people are added to the contributing team and as the team is broadened to help realize its true value. Throughout, we remain consistent with PSI as it evolves based on its development project. This chapter presents one temporary closure.

2. The problem space is the translation of the design intent. Design intent leads to addressing a particular problem or need that has been identified—a purposeful

exercise. For example, the problem of how I move from A to B is driven by the desire to move from A to B.

3. The case study of Convers[t]ation is based on the first edition of the Design across Cultures project, a collaboration between Fields of View, Bangalore, and MediaLAB, Amsterdam. More details on the project can be found at http://fieldsofview.in/projects/converstation. Sruthi Krishnan was part of the project.

4. The strategic plan of the Carnegie Mellon University Engineering Design Research Center (1986–1997) included a characterization of design situations with seven dimensions that have some overlap with the dimensions of the PSI framework but without identifying the three separate spaces.

5. The problem space encompasses the product or artifact being designed, which evolves during the design process. The current understanding of the artifact is captured in the theory of the artifact. In design, our understanding of the problem and our understanding the artifact coevolve as the dialogue progresses. See D. Braha and Y. Reich, "Topological Structures for Modeling Engineering Design Processes," *Research in Engineering Design* 14, no. 4 (2003): 185–199.

6. For example, Japanese automobile companies have four tiers of supplier relationships that vary from suppliers who provide commodity parts (weak) to those who are intricately involved (strong) with the parent company in design and manufacture of subsystems. Rajan R. Kamath and Jeffrey K. Liker, "A Second Look at Japanese Product Development," *Harvard Business Review* 72 (1994): 154–173. An approach to designing such as sequential engineering embodies a weak relationship among the design, marketing, and manufacturing functions in a company, whereas concurrent engineering implies strong ties between these functional roles within a company. Kim B. Clark and Takahiro Fujimoto, *Product Development Performance: Strategy, Organization, and Management in the World Auto Industry* (Boston: Harvard Business Press, 1991).

7. It is sometimes said that if a company could know what it knows, it would perform much better. Many efforts in knowledge management were attempts to bridge this gap through technology, but they often were insufficient because they relate to short-term and long-term knowledge (shared memory) and their nurture is beyond pure technological means. Joseph G. Davis, Eswaran Subrahmanian, and Arthur W. Westerberg, "The 'Global' and the 'Local' in Knowledge Management," *Journal of Knowledge Management* 9, no. 1 (2005): 101–112.

8. Edward Lorenz makes the case that distributed cognition based on the cultural-historical perspective explains issues in knowledge and organizational theory that go beyond information processing and the situated cognition perspectives. Distributed cognition explains organizational routines, learning, and team-based problem solving that are mediated through cognitive artifacts in the cultural-historical processes situated in a context. In the case of designing, this is even more important because cognitive artifacts are created, modified, and mediated through the shared memory of the team, socialization through apprenticeships, and their cultural-historical origin. Edward Lorenz, "Models of Cognition, the Contextualisation of Knowledge

and Organisational Theory," *Journal of Management and Governance* 5, no. 3–4 (2001): 307–330.

9. Shilpa Phadke, Sameera Khan, and Shilpa Ranade, *Why Loiter? Women and Risk on Mumbai Streets* (Delhi: Penguin Books India, 2011).

10. We see here a clear example of how the change in the problem definition leads to questioning of the validity of the proposed solution product, demonstrating the coevolution of the problem and product spaces.

11. Had the project ended with a panic button product, it could have caused significant damage, exemplifying many other economic development projects that suffer from the same misaligned PSI spaces. For additional analysis and examples, see E. Subrahmanian, C. Eckert, C. McMahon, and Y. Reich, "Economic Development as Design: Insight and Guidance through the PSI Framework," in *Proceedings of the Twenty-first International Conference on Engineering Design (ICED 17)*, Vancouver, Canada, August 21–25, pp. 229–238 (Glasgow: Design Society, 2017).

12. Groupthink is a psychological phenomenon related to group decision making in which groups try to arrive quickly at a consensus without seriously considering alternatives or critical information from outside the group. Irving L. Janis, *Victims of Groupthink: A Psychological Study of Foreign-Policy Decisions and Fiascoes* (Boston: Houghton Mifflin, 1972).

13. "Data Busts Some Myths on Sexual Violence," *The Hindu*, September 3, 2013, http://www.thehindu.com/news/national/data-busts-some-myths-on-sexual-vio lence/article5089690.ece (accessed December 28, 2018).

14. We see now that the PSI framework not only helps characterize the present situation and indicate where to go in the future for further development or alignment but also serves as a decision-making tool to determine whether a project needs to be deferred because the available resources and perhaps knowledge are not available to lead to a successful completion.

15. Indrani Medhi-Thies, "User Interface Design for Low-Literate and Novice Users: Past, Present and Future," *Foundations and Trends in Human-Computer Interaction* 8, no. 1 (2015): 1–72; Indrani Medhi-Thies, Pedro Ferreira, Nakull Gupta, Jacki O'Neill, Edward Cutrell, and Krishi Pustak, "A Social Networking System for Low-Literate Farmers," *Proceedings of the Eighteenth ACM Conference on Computer-Supported Cooperative Work*, Vancouver, March 14–18, 2015 (New York: Association for Computing Machinery, 2015).

16. In an influential article, Linda Argote and Paul Ingram write that knowledge transfer is difficult within an organization and but that "knowledge embedded in the interactions of people, tools, and tasks provides a basis for competitive advantage in firms." Linda Argote and Paul Ingram, "Knowledge Transfer: A Basis for Competitive Advantage in Firms," *Organizational Behavior and Human Decision Processes* 82, no. 1 (2000): 150–169. This work supports our claim that the status of the theory of artifact that is maintained by internal interactions and dialogues determines the health of the process of designing and hence the competitive advantage of the organization.

Chapter 7

1. Roberto Mangabeira Unger, *The Self Awakened: Pragmatism Unbound* (Cambridge, MA: Harvard University Press, 2007), 7.
2. Unger, *The Self Awakened*, 57.
3. Unger, *The Self Awakened*, 57.
4. Slavoj Žižek, *Welcome to the Desert of the Real! Five Essays on September 11 and Related Dates* (New York: Verso, 2002), 1.
5. Tomas Hachard, "The Red Ink," *Guernica*, June 4, 2012, https://www.guernica mag.com/daily/tomas-hachard-the-red-ink (accessed July 4, 2016).
6. Žižek, *Welcome to the Desert of the Real*, 2.
7. Paulo Freire, *Pedagogy of the Oppressed* (1970) (New York: Bloomsbury, 2018).
8. Chimamanda Ngozi Adichie, "The Danger of a Single Story," TEDGlobal 2009, http://www.ted.com/talks/chimamanda_adichie_the_danger_of_a_single_story/transcript?language=en.
9. Edward O. Wilson, *Naturalist* (Washington, DC: Island Press, 2006), 364.

Appendix B

1. See Joseph G. Davis, Eswaran Subrahmanian, Sureah Konda, Helen Granger, Michael Collins, and Arthur W. Westerberg, "Creating Shared Information Spaces to Support Collaborative Design Work," *Information Systems Frontiers* 3 no. 3 (2001): 377–392; Philip Sargent, Eswaran Subrahmanian, Mary Downs, Reid Greene, and Diane Rishel. "Materials' Information and Conceptual Data Modelling," in *Computerization and Networking of Materials Databases*. Vol. 3, *STP 1140*, ed. Thomas I. Barry and Keith W. Reynaud (Philadelphia: American Society for Testing and Materials, 1992), 172; Eswaran Subrahmanian, "Study of Reuse in Switchgear Design: An Information Flow Analysis Based Study at ABB Distribution at Skein," ABB R&D Report. ABB Corporate Research, Norway, June 1995; Eswaran Subrahmanian and Ellen Daleng, "Information Flow Analysis of Hydro Power Design at Drummen," ABB R&D Report. ABB Corporate Research, Norway, 1993; Eswaran Subrahmanian, Susan Finger, and Tom Mitchell, "A Report on the NSF-EDRC Study of Product Design Processes in Selected Japanese Companies," EDRC Research Report 05-75-93, Energy Design Research Center, Carnegie-Mellon University, Pittsburgh, 1993; Eswaran Subrahmanian, Helen Granger, and Russ Milliken, "A Report on the Study of the Design and Engineering Change Process at Adtranz," November 2000; Eswaran Subrahmanian, Andrea Jahnke, Harald Mackamul, and Thomas Schwab, "Information Flow Analysis of Product Development at Bosch Power Tools at Leinfelden," Robert Bosch R&D Report, Robert Bosch Corporate R&D, Schillerhoe, June 1997; Eswaran Subrahmanian and Edgar Jellum, "Total Plant Engineering: An Information Flow Study of Total Power Plant Engineering at ABB," ABB R&D Report, ABB Corporate Research, Norway, May 1998; and Eswaran Subrahmanian, Christopher Lee, and Helen Granger, "Managing and Supporting Product Life Cycle through Engineering Change Management for a Complex Product," *Research in Engineering Design* 26, no. 3 (2015): 189–217.

Bibliography

Addis, William. *Structural Engineering: The Nature of Theory and Design*. Hemels, UK: Ellis Horwood, 1990.

Adichi, Chimamanda Ngozi. "The Danger of a Single Story." TED Talk, TEDGlobal 2009. http://www.ted.com/talks/chimamanda_adichie_the_danger_of_a_single_story/transcript?language=en.

Agence France-Press in Addis Ababa. "Death Toll from Rubbish Dump Landslide in Ethiopia Rises to Sixty-Five." *The Guardian*, March 13, 2017. https://www.theguardian.com/world/2017/mar/13/death-toll-rises-to-65-after-rubbish-dump-landslide-in-ethiopia (accessed December 28, 2018).

Agre, P. E. "Hierarchy and History in Simon's 'Architecture of Complexity.'" *Journal of the Learning Sciences* 12, no. 3 (2003): 413–426.

Alexander, Christopher. *A Pattern Language: Towns, Buildings, Construction*. New York: Oxford University Press, 1977.

Argote, Linda, and Paul Ingram. "Knowledge Transfer: A Basis for Competitive Advantage in Firms." *Organizational Behavior and Human Decision Processes* 82, no. 1 (2000): 150–169.

Ball, Linden J., and Thomas C. Ormerod. "Putting Ethnography to Work: The Case for a Cognitive Ethnography of Design." *International Journal of Human-Computer Studies* 53, no. 1 (2000): 147–168.

Basalla, George. *The Evolution of Technology*. New York: Cambridge University Press, 1988.

Baudrillard, Jean. *Simulacra and Simulation*. Ann Arbor: University of Michigan Press, 1994.

Bayazit, Nigan. "Investigating Design: A Review of Forty Years of Design Research." *Design Issues* 20, no. 1 (2004): 21–22.

Berger, John. *Ways of Seeing*. London: Penguin, 2008.

Bhavnani, Suresh K., and Bonnie E. John. "The Strategic Use of Complex Computer Systems." *Human-Computer Interaction* 15, no. 2 (2000): 107–137.

Bohman, James. "Critical Theory." In *The Stanford Encyclopedia of Philosophy*, fall 2016 ed., edited by Edward N. Zalta, March 8, 2005. https://plato_stanford.ed/entries/critical-theory (accessed December 28, 2018).

Borges, Jorge Luis, *Labyrinths: Selected Stories and Other Writings*, edited by Donald A. Yates and James E. Irby. London: Penguin, 2000.

Bowker, Geoffrey C., and Susan Leigh Star. *Sorting Things Out: Classification and Its Consequences*. Cambridge, MA: MIT Press, 2000.

Braha, Daniel, and Yoram Reich. "Topological Structures for Modeling Engineering Design Processes." *Research in Engineering Design* 14, no. 4 (2003): 185–199.

Brooks, Frederick P. *The Mythical Man-Month: Essays on Software Engineering*, 2nd ed. Reading, MA: Addison-Wesley, 1995.

Bucciarelli, Louis L. *Designing Engineers*. Cambridge, MA: MIT Press, 1994.

Bucciarelli, Louis L. *Engineering Philosophy*. Delft: Dup Satellite, 2003.

Bucciarelli, Louis L. "An Ethnographic Perspective on Engineering Design." *Design Studies* 9, no. 3 (1988): 159–168.

Buchanan, Richard. "Rhetoric, Humanism, and Design." In *Discovering Design: Explorations in Design Studies*, edited by Richard Buchanan and Victor Margolin, 23–66. Chicago: University of Chicago Press, 1995.

Buchanan, Richard, and Victor Margolin, eds. *Discovering Design: Explorations in Design Studies*. Chicago: University of Chicago Press, 1995.

Buchanan, Richard, and Victor Margolin, eds. *The Idea of Design: A* Design Issues *Reader*. Cambridge, MA: MIT Press, 1995.

Bürdek, Bernhard E. *Design: History, Theory and Practice of Product Design*. Basel: Birkhauser Architecture, 2005.

Busby, J. S. "Error and Distributed Cognition in Design." *Design Studies* 22, no. 3 (2001): 233–254.

Bush, Vannevar. "Science: The Endless Frontier." *Transactions of the Kansas Academy of Science (1903–)* 48, no. 3 (1945): 231–264.

Capra, Frizhoff. *Web of Life: A New Scientific Understanding of Living Systems*. New York: Anchor, 1997.

Calvino, Italo. *Mr. Palomar*. Translated by William Weaver. London: Vintage, [1983] 1999.

Chakraberty, Sumit. "From Waste Picker to Recycling Manager." Citiscope, April 14, 2014. http://archive.citiscope.org/story/2014/waste-picker-recycling-manager (accessed December 28, 2018).

Chandran, Pinky, Nalini Shekar, Marwan Abubaker, and Aksay Yadav. "Informal Waste Workers Contribution Bangalore." Working paper, Jain University, Bangalore, India, August 1, 2016. http://hasirudala.in/wp-content/uploads/2016/08/1.-Full-Paper-Chandran-Informal-Waste-Workers-Contribution-in-Bangalore-1.pdf (accessed December 28, 2018).

Chater, Nick, and Morten H. Christiansen. "Language Acquisition Meets Language Evolution." *Cognitive Science* 34, no. 7 (2010): 1131–1157.

Clancey, William J. *Working on Mars: Voyages of Scientific Discovery with the Mars Exploration Rovers.* Cambridge, MA: MIT Press, 2012.

Clark, Andy. *Being There: Putting Brain, Body, and World Together Again.* Cambridge, MA: MIT Press, 1998.

Clark, Herbert H. *Using Language.* Cambridge: Cambridge University Press, 1996.

Clark, Kim B., and Takahiro Fujimoto. *Product Development Performance: Strategy, Organization, and Management in the World Auto Industry.* Boston: Harvard Business Press, 1991.

Cross, Nigel. *Engineering Design Methods.* Chichester: Wiley, 1989.

Cross, Nigel. "A History of Design Methodology." In *Design Methodology and Relationships with Science*, edited by M. J de Vries, N. Cross, and D. P. Grant, 15–27. Dordrecht: Springer Science, 1993.

Davis, Joseph G., Eswaran Subrahmanian, Sureah Konda, Helen Granger, Michael Collins, and Arthur W. Westerberg. "Creating Shared Information Spaces to Support Collaborative Design Work." *Information Systems Frontiers* 3 no. 3 (2001): 377–392.

Davis, Joseph G., Eswaran Subrahmanian, and Arthur W. Westerbery. "The 'Global' and the 'Local' in Knowledge Management." *Journal of Knowledge Management* 9, no. 1 (2005): 101–112.

Deforge, Yves. "Avatars of Design: Design before Design." In *The Idea of Design: A Design Issues Reader*, edited by Richard Buchanan and Victor Margolin, 21–28. Cambridge, MA: MIT Press, 1995.

Deming, W. Edwards. *The New Economics for Industry, Government, Education.* Cambridge, MA: Massachusetts Institute of Technology, Center for Advanced Educational Services, 1994.

Easterly, William. *The Elusive Quest for Growth: Economists' Adventures and Misadventures in the Tropics.* Cambridge, MA: MIT Press, 2001.

Easterly, William. *Tyranny of Experts*. New York: Basic Books, 2014.

Environment Support Group. "Bangalore's Toxic Legacy Intensifies: Status of Landfills, Waste Processing Sites and Dumping Grounds, and Working Conditions of Pourakarmikas, Bangalore, India." http://www.indiaenvironmentportal.org.in/files/file/bangalore-s-toxic-legacy-intensifies.pdf (accessed December 28, 2018).

Ferguson, Eugene S. *Engineering and the Mind's Eye*. Cambridge, MA: MIT Press, 1994.

Fields of View. "Rubbish!" Bangalore, India, 2017. http://fieldsofview.in/projects/rubbish.

Fields of View. "White Paper Documenting the Process of Designing Convers[t] ation." 2014. http://fieldsofview.in/publications/visuals/WhitePaperConverstation 2014 (accessed December 28, 2018).

Fields of View. "White Paper on Rubbish!" http://fieldsofview.in/publications/visuals/WhitePaperOnTheGameRubbish (accessed December 28, 2018).

Findeli, Alain. "Moholy-Nagy's Design Pedagogy in Chicago (1937–46)." In *The Idea of Design: A Design Issues Reader*, edited by Richard Buchanan and Victor Margolin, 29–43. Cambridge, MA: MIT Press, 1995.

Finger, Susan, Eswaran Subrahmanian, and Eric Gardner. "A Design System for Concurrent Engineering of Transformers." In *Proceedings of ICED93 / Ninth International Conference on Engineering Design*, August 17–19, 1993, The Hague. Zurich: Heurista, 1993.

Flemming, Ulrich, Suresh K. Bhavnani, and Bonnie E. John. "Mismatched Metaphor: User vs System Model in Computer-Aided Drafting." *Design Studies* 18, no. 4 (1997): 349–368.

Floridi, Luciano. *The Philosophy of Information*. Oxford: Oxford University Press, 2011.

Freire, Paulo. *Pedagogy of the Oppressed*. New York: Bloomsbury, 2018.

Frigg, Roland, and Steven Hartmann. "Scientific Models." In *The Philosophy of Science: An Encyclopedia*, vol. 2, edited by Sahotra Sarkar and Jessica Pfeifer. New York: Routledge, 2005.

Gardner, Howard. *Five Minds for the Future*. Boston: Harvard Business Press, 2006.

Giere, Ronald. "Scientific Cognition as Distributed Cognition." In *The Cognitive Basis of Science*, edited by Peter Carruthers, Stephen Stich, and Michael Siegal, 285–299. New York: Cambridge University Press, 2002.

Giere, Ronald N. "Using Models to Represent Reality." In *Model-Based Reasoning in Scientific Discovery*, edited by Magnani, Lorenzo, Nancy J. Nersessian, and Paul Thagard, 41–57. New York: Kluwer/Plenum, 1999.

Ghemawat, Pankaj, *Redefining Global Strategy: Crossing Borders in a World Where Differences Still Matter*. Cambridge, MA: Harvard University Press, 2007.

Goldwater, Robert John, and Marco Treves, eds. *Artists on Art: From the Fourteenth to the Twentieth Century*. New York: Pantheon, 1945.

Gropius, Walter. *Scope of Total Architecture*. London: G. Allen & Unwin, 1956. As cited in *Discovering Design: Explorations in Design Studies*, edited by Richard Buchanan and Victor Margolin. Chicago: University of Chicago Press, 1995.

Hatchuel, Armand, Pascal Le Masson, Yoram Reich, and Eswaran Subrahmanian. "Design Theory: The Foundations of a New Paradigm for Science and Engineering." *Research in Engineering Design* 29, no. 1 (2018): 5–21.

Hatchuel, Armand, and Benoit Weil. "C-K Design Theory: An Advanced Formulation." *Research in Engineering Design* 19, no. 4 (2009): 181–192.

Hatchuel, Armand, and Benoit Weil. "A New Approach of Innovative Design: An Introduction to CK Theory." In *DS 31: Proceedings of ICED 03, the Fourteenth International Conference on Engineering Design*, Stockholm. Glasgow: Design Society, 2003.

Heiser, Julie, Barbara Tversky, and Mia Silverman. "Sketches for and from Collaboration." In *Third International Conference on Visual and Spatial Reasoning in Design*, edited by John S. Gero, Barbara Tversky, and Terry Knight, 69–78. Sydney: Key Centre of Design Computing and Cognition University, 2004.

Henderson, Kathryn. *On Line and on Paper: Visual Representations, Visual Culture, and Computer Graphics in Design Engineering*. Cambridge, MA: MIT Press, 1999.

Hillier, Bill, John Musgrave, and Pat O'Sullivan. "Knowledge and Design." In *Environmental Design: Research and Practice*, edited by William J. Mitchell, 29.3.1–29.3.14. Los Angeles: University of California, 1972.

Hubka, Vladimir, and W. Ernst Eder. *Design Science: Introduction to the Needs, Scope and Organization of Engineering Design Knowledge*. London: Springer, 1996.

Hubka, Vladimir, and W. Ernst Eder. "A Scientific Approach to Engineering Design." *Design Studies* 8, no. 3 (1987): 123–137.

Hubka, Vladimir, and W. Ernst Eder. *Theory of Technical Systems: A Total Concept Theory for Engineering Design*. London: Springer, 1988.

Hutchins, Edwin. *Cognition in the Wild*. Cambridge, MA: MIT Press, 1995.

Hutchins, Edwin. "Distributed Cognition." In *International Encyclopedia of the Social and Behavioral Sciences*, edited by Neil J. Sonelse and Paul B. Baltes, 2068–2072. Oxford: Elsevier Science, 2001.

Hutchins, Edwin. "How a Cockpit Remembers Its Speeds." *Cognitive Science* 19, no. 3 (1995): 265–288.

Janis, Irving L. *Victims of Groupthink: A Psychological Study of Foreign-Policy Decisions and Fiascoes*. Boston: Houghton Mifflin, 1972.

Jones, J. Christopher. "How My Thoughts about Design Methods Have Changed during the Years." *Design Methods and Theories* 11, no. 1 (1977): 48–62.

Kamath, Rajan R., and Jeffrey K. Liker. "A Second Look at Japanese Product Development." *Harvard Business Review* 72 (1994): 154–173.

Keene, Courtney. "Development Projects That Did Not Work: The Perils of Narrow Approaches to Complex Problems." Globalhood research report, 2007. http://newmajoritylabs.com/wp-content/uploads/2015/11/Development_Projects_That_Didnt_Work.pdf (accessed July 3, 2016).

Konda, Suresh, Ira Monarch, Philip Sargent, and Eswaran Subrahmanian. "Shared Memory in Design: A Unifying Theme for Research and Practice." *Research in Engineering Design* 4 no. 1 (1992): 23–42.

Krishnan, Sruthi. "Scaling the Mountainous Problem of Garbage." *The Hindu*, May 4, 2017. http://www.thehindu.com/thread/politics-and-policy/when-mountains-of-garbage-come-crashing-down/article18383260.ece (accessed December 28, 2018).

Kunz, Werner, and Horst W. J. Rittel. "Issues as Elements of Information Systems." Working Paper 131. Institute of Urban and Regional Development, University of California at Berkeley, 1970.

Lakoff, George. *Don't Think of an Elephant! Know Your Values and Frame the Debate: The Essential Guide for Progressives.* White River Junction, VT: Chelsea Green, 2004.

Lave, Jean, and Etienne Wenger. *Communities of Practice: Learning, Meaning, and Identity.* Cambridge: Cambridge University Press, 1998.

Lave, Jean, and Etienne Wenger. *Situated Learning: Legitimate Peripheral Participation.* Cambridge: Cambridge University Press, 1991.

Le Masson, Pascal, Armand Hatchuel, and Benoit Weil. "Design Theory at Bauhaus: Teaching 'Splitting' Knowledge." *Research in Engineering Design* 27, no. 2 (2016): 91–115.

Lorenz, Edward. "Models of Cognition, the Contextualisation of Knowledge and Organisational Theory." *Journal of Management and Governance* 5, no. 3–4 (2001): 307–330.

Magnani, Lorenzo, and Nancy J. Nersessian. *Model-Based Reasoning: Science, Technology, Values.* London: Springer, 2002.

Medhi-Thies, Indrani. "User Interface Design for Low-Literate and Novice Users: Past, Present and Future." *Foundations and Trends in Human-Computer Interaction* 8, no. 1 (2015): 1–72.

Medhi-Thies, Indrani, Pedro Ferreira, Nakull Gupta, Jacki O'Neill, Edward Cutrell, and Krishi Pustak. "A Social Networking System for Low-Literate Farmers." In *Proceedings of the Eighteenth ACM Conference on Computer-Supported Cooperative Work,*

Vancouver, March 14–18, 2015. New York: Association for Computing Machinery, 2015.

Meijer, Sebastian, Yoram Reich, and Eswaran Subrahmanian. "The Future of Gaming for Design of Complex Systems." In *Back to the Future of Gaming*, edited by Richard D. Duke and Willy C. Kriz, 154–167. Bielefeld: W. Bertelsmann, 2014.

Miller, Daniel. "Designing Ourselves." In *Design Anthropology: Object Culture in the Twenty-first Century*, 88–99. New York: Springer, 2011.

Mitchell, Melanie. *Complexity: A Guided Tour*. New York: Oxford University Press, 2009.

Mokyr, Joel. *The Gifts of Athena: Historical Origins of the Knowledge Economy*. Princeton, NJ: Princeton University Press, 2002.

Monarch, Ira, Suresh L. Konda, Sean N, Levy, Yoram Reich, Eswaran Subrahmanian, and Carol Ulrich. "Mapping Sociotechnical Networks in the Making." In *Social Science, Technical Systems, and Cooperative Work: Beyond the Great Divide*, edited by Geoffrey C. Bowker, Susan Leigh Star, William Turner, and Les Gasser, 331–354. Mahwah, NJ: Erlbaum, 1997.

Morgan, Mary S., and Margaret Morrison. *Models as Mediators: Perspectives on Natural and Social Science*. Cambridge: Cambridge University Press, 1999.

Morin, Edgar. "Restricted Complexity, General Complexity." In *Worldviews, Science and Us: Philosophy and Complexity*, edited by Carlos Gershenson, Diederik Aerts, and Bruce Edmonds, 5–29. Singapore: World Scientific Publishing, 2007.

National Institutes of Health. "NIH Human Microbiome Project Defines Normal Bacterial Makeup of the Body," news release, June 13, 2012. http://www.nih.gov/news/health/jun2012/nhgri-13.htm (accessed July 26, 2015).

Narayanamurti, Venkatesh, Tolu Odumosu, and Lee Vinsel. "RIP: The Basic/Applied Research Dichotomy." *Issues in Science and Technology* 29, no. 2 (2013): 31–36.

Newell, Allen, and Herbert A. Simon. *Human Problem Solving*. Englewood Cliffs, NJ: Prentice-Hall, 1972.

Nisbett, Richard. *The Geography of Thought: How Asians and Westerners Think Differently ... and Why*. New York: Simon and Schuster, 2004, 20.

Norman, Donald. "Why Design Education Must Change." *Core77*, November 26,2010.http://www.core77.com/blog/columns/why_design_edcation_must_change_17993.asp.

Page, Scott E. *The Difference: How the Power of Diversity Creates Better Groups, Firms, Schools, and Societies*. Princeton, NJ: Princeton University Press, 2008.

Pahl, Gerhard, Wolfgang Beitz, Jorg Feldhusen, and Karl-Heinrich Grote. *Engineering Design: A Systematic Approach*. 3rd ed. London: Springer, 2007.

Petroski, Henry. *Design Paradigms: Case Histories of Error and Judgment in Engineering*. Cambridge: Cambridge University Press, 1994.

Petroski, Henry. *Success through Failure: The Paradox of Design*. Princeton, NJ: Princeton University Press, 2006.

Phadke, Shilpa, Sameera Khan, and Shilpa Ranade. *Why Loiter? Women and Risk on Mumbai Streets*. Delhi: Penguin Books India, 2011.

Pirtle, Zachary. "How the Models of Engineering Tell the Truth." *Philosophy of Engineering and Technology*. Vol. 2. Basel: Springer Science +Business Media, 2010.

Portugali, Juval. *Complexity, Cognition and the City*. New York: Springer, 2011.

Reddy, Jayachandra M., Susan Finger, Suresh Konda, and Eswaran Subrahmanian. "Design as Building and Reusing Artifact Theories: Understanding and Supporting Growth of Design Knowledge." In *The Design Productivity Debate*, edited by Alex H. B. Duffy, 268–290. London: Springer, 1998.

Reich, Yoram. "A Critical Review of General Design Theory." *Research in Engineering Design* 7, no. 1 (1995): 1–18.

Reich, Yoram. "Transcending the Theory-Practice Problem of Technology." EDRC Report 12-51-92. Engineering Design Research Center, Carnegie Mellon University, Pittsburgh, 1992.

Reich, Yoram, Suresh L Konda., Ira A. Monarch, Sean N. Levy, and Eswaran Subrahmanian. "Varieties and Issues of Participation and Design." *Design Studies* 17, no. 2 (1996): 165–180.

Reich, Yoram, Suresh L. Konda, Eswaran Subrahmanian, Douglas Cunningham, Allen Dutoit, Robert Patrick, Mark Thomas, and Arthur W. Westerberg. "Building Agility for Developing Agile Design Information Systems." *Research in Engineering Design* 11, no. 2 (1999): 67–83.

Reich, Yoram, Offer Shai, Eswaran Subrahmanian, Armand Hatchuel, and Pascal Le Masson. "The Interplay between Design and Mathematics: Introduction to Bootstrapping Effects." In *Proceedings of the Ninth Biennial Conference on Engineering Systems Design and Analysis (ASME 2008)*, 223–228. New York: American Society of Mechanical Engineers, 2008.

Reich, Yoram, and Eswaran Subrahmanian. "The PSI Matrix: A Framework and a Theory of Design." In *Proceedings of the Twenty-first International Conference on Engineering Design ICED 17*, Vancouver, August 21–25, 2017, edited by Anja Maier, Stanko Skec, Chris McKesson, and Mike Van de Loos. Glasgow: Design Society, 2017.

Rittel, Horst W. J., and Melvin M. Webber. "Dilemmas in a General Theory of Planning." *Policy Sciences* 4, no. 2 (1973): 155–169.

Rosenberg, Nathan. "Charles Babbage: Pioneer Economist." In *Exploring the Black Box: Technology, Economics and History*, 24–46. Cambridge: Cambridge University Press, 1994.

Sainath, Palagummi. *Everybody Loves a Good Drought: Stories from India's Poorest Districts*. Delhi: Penguin Books India, 1996.

Sargent Philip, Eswaran Subrahmanian, Mary Downs, Reid Greene, and Diane Rishel. "Materials' Information and Conceptual Data Modelling." In *Computerization and Networking of Materials Databases*. Vol. 3, *STP 1140*, edited by Thomas I. Barry and Keith W. Reynaud, 172. Philadelphia: American Society for Testing and Materials, 1992.

Savage, Dwayne C. "Microbial Ecology of the Gastrointestinal Trace." *Annual Reviews in Microbiology* 31, no. 1 (1997): 107–133.

Schauder, Stephan, and Bonnie L. Bassler. "The Languages of Bacteria." *Genes & Development* 15, no. 12 (2001): 1468–1480.

Schön, Donald A. *The Reflective Practitioner: How Professionals Think in Action*. New York: Basic Books, 1983.

Seibert, Brian. "Stillness and Motion and Voluptuous Curves, in a Temple Setting." Dance review. *New York Times*, January 12, 2015. http://www.nytimes.com/2015/01/13/arts/dance/nrityagram-dancers-at-the-temple-of-dendur-at-the-met.html?_r=0.

Sen, Amartya. *Identity and Violence: The Illusion of Destiny*. Delhi: Penguin Books India, 2007.

Shneiderman, Ben. *The New ABCs of Research: Achieving Breakthrough Collaborations*. Oxford: Oxford University Press, 2016.

Simon, Herbert A. "From Substantive to Procedural Rationality." In *Twenty-five Years of Economic Theory: Retrospect and Prospect*, edited by T. J. Kastelei, S. K. Kuipers, W. A. Nijenhuis, and G. R. Wagenaar, 65–86. Boston: Martinus Nijhoff Social Sciences Division, 1976.

Simon, Herbert A. *The Sciences of the Artificial*. Cambridge, MA: MIT Press, 1981.

Smith, Adam. *The Wealth of Nations*. Vol. 3, edited by Andrew S. Skinner. New York: Prometheus Books, 1991.

Srinivasan, Meera. "When a Trash Mountain Spelt Tragedy." *The Hindu*, April 22, 2017. https://www.thehindu.com/todays-paper/tp-international/when-a-trash-mountain-spelt-tragedy/article18193670.ece (accessed December 28, 2018).

Star, Susan Leigh, and James R. Griesemer. "Institutional Ecology, 'Translations' and Boundary Objects: Amateurs and Professionals in Berkeley's Museum of Vertebrate Zoology, 1907–39." *Social Studies of Science* 19, no. 3 (1989): 387–420.

Subrahmanian, Eswaran. "Study of Reuse in Switchgear Design: An Information Flow Analysis Based Study at ABB Distribution at Skein." ABB R&D Report. ABB Corporate Research, Norway, June 1995.

Subrahmanian, Eswaran, and Ellen Daleng, "Information Flow Analysis of Hydro Power Design at Drummen." ABB R&D Report. ABB Corporate Research, Norway, 1993.

Subrahmanian, Eswaran, Claudia Eckert, Christopher McMahon, and Yoram Reich. "Economic Development as Design: Insight and Guidance through the PSI Framework." In *Proceedings of ICED 17, the Twenty-first International Conference on Engineering*, Vancouver, August 21–25, 2017, 229–238. Glasgow: Design Society, 2017.

Subrahmanian, Eswaran, Susan Finger, and Tom Mitchell. "A Report on the NSF-EDRC Study of Product Design Processes in Selected Japanese Companies." EDRC Research Report 05-75-93. Energy Design Research Center, Carnegie-Mellon University, Pittsburgh, 1993.

Subrahmanian, Eswaran, Helen Granger, and Russ Milliken. "A Report on the Study of the Design and Engineering Change Process at Adtranz." November 2000.

Subrahmanian, Eswaran, Andrea Jahnke, Harald Mackamul, and Thomas Schwab. "Information Flow Analysis of Product Development at Bosch Power Tools at Leinfelden." Robert Bosch R&D Report. Robert Bosch Corporate R&D, Schillerhoe, June 1997.

Subrahmanian, Eswaran, and Edgar Jellum. "Total Plant Engineering: An Information Flow Study of Total Power Plant Engineering at ABB." ABB R&D Report. ABB Corporate Research, Norway, May 1998.

Subrahmanian, Eswaran, Suresh L. Konda, Sean L. Levy, Yoram Reich, Arthur W. Westerberg, and Ira Monarch. "Equations Aren't Enough: Informal Modelling in Design." *AI EDAM* 7, no. 4 (1993): 257–274.

Subrahmanian, Eswaran, Christopher Lee, and Helen Granger. "Managing and Supporting Product Life Cycle through Engineering Change Management for a Complex Product." *Research in Engineering Design* 26, no. 3 (2015): 189–217.

Subrahmanian, Eswaran, Yoram Reich, Smulders Frido, and Sebastian A. Meijer. "Design as a Synthesis of Spaces: Using the P-S Framework." In *Proceedings of IASDR2011, the Fourth World Conference in Design Research*, Delft, The Netherlands, 2011. International Association of Societies of Design Research, 2011.

Subrahmanian, Eswaran, Yoram Reich, Smulders Frido, and Sebastian A. Meijer. "Designing: Insights from Weaving Theories of Cognition and Design Theories. In *Proceedings of the Eighteenth International Conference on Engineering Design (ICED 11)*, Copenhagen, Denmakr, 2011. Glasgow: Design Society.

Subrahmanian, Eswaran, Yoram Reich, Suresh L. Konda, Allen Dutoit, Douglas Cunningham, Robert Patrick, Mark Thomas, and Arthur W. Westerberg. "The *n*-Dim Approach to Creating Design Support Systems." In *Proceedings of the 1997 ASME Design Engineering Technical Conferences: DETC '97*. New York: American Society of Mechanical Engineers, 1997.

Subrahmanian, E., A. W. Westerberg, and G. Podnar. "Towards Shared Information Models in Engineering Design." In *Lecture Notes in Collaborative Product Development*, edited by Duvvuru Sriram. London: Springer, 1991.

Suchman, Lucy A. *Plans and Situated Actions: The Problem of Human-Machine Communication*. Cambridge: Cambridge University Press, 1987.

Suwa, Masaki, and Barbara Tversky. "What Do Architects and Students Perceive in Their Design Sketches? A Protocol Analysis." *Design Studies* 18, no. 4 (1997): 385–403.

Tagore, Rabindranath. *Fruit Gathering*. In *The Project Gutenberg*, 2009. https://www.gutenberg.org/ebooks/6522 (accessed May 3, 2019).

Tagore, Rabindranath. *Gitanjali*. New Delhi: UBS Publishing Distributors, 2003.

Tomasello, Michael. *The Cultural Origins of Human Cognition*. Cambridge, MA: Harvard University Press, 2009.

Tomiyama, Tetsuo, and Hiroshi Yoshikawa. "Extended General Design Theory." Technical Report CS-R8604. Amsterdam: Centre for Mathematics and Computer Science, 1986.

Unger, Roberto Mangabeira. *The Self Awakened: Pragmatism Unbound*. Cambridge, MA: Harvard University Press, 2007.

Varela, Francisco, Eleanor Rosch, and Evan Thompson. *The Embodied Mind: Cognitive Science and Human Experience*. Cambridge, MA: MIT Press, 1991.

Verma, Jagdish Sharan, Leila Seth, and Gopal Subramanian. "Report of the Committee on Amendments to Criminal Law, 2013." New Delhi: PRS Legislative Research, 2013.

Visser, Willemien. "Designing as Construction of Representations: A Dynamic Viewpoint in Cognitive Design Research." *Human–Computer Interaction* 21, no. 1 (2006): 103–152.

Vitruvius. *The Ten Books on Architecture*. Translated by Morris Hickey Morgan. Cambridge, MA: Harvard University Press, 1914. In *The Project Gutenberg*, 2006. http://www.gutenberg.org/files/20239/20239-h/29239-h.htm (accessed December 2, 2018).

Wijesiriwardena, Subha. "What *Samhara* Means: A Review of *Samhara* and an Unraveling of What It Really Means for Sri Lankan Dance." Blog, May 16, 2012. https://blogsmw.wordpress.com/2012/05/16/what-samhara-means-a-review-of-samhara-and-an-unraveling-of-what-it-really-means-for-sri-lankan-dance (accessed July 5, 2016).

Wilson, Edward O. *Naturalist*. Washington, DC: Island Press, 2006.

Yoshikawa, Hiroyuki. "General Design Theory and a CAD System." In *Man-Machine Communication in CAD/CAM, Proceedings of the IFIP WG5.2–5.3 Working Conference Held in Tokyo, Japan, October 2–4, 1980*, edited by Toshio Sata and Ernest Warman, 35–57. Amsterdam: North-Holland, 1981.

Ziman, John. "Emerging out of Nature into History: The Plurality of the Sciences." *Philosophical Transactions of the Royal Society of London A: Mathematical, Physical and Engineering Sciences* 361, no. 1809 (2003): 1617–1633.

Ziman, John. "Is Science Losing Its Objectivity?" *Nature* 382, no. 6594 (1996): 751–754.

Žižek, Slavoj. *Welcome to the Desert of the Real! Five Essays on September 11 and Related Dates*. New York: Verso, 2002.

Index